100 Contemporary Christian Poets

This selection contains poems by 100 contemporary poets – some well known, others as yet unknown. Almost all the poems are previously unpublished.

It is not a book of 'religious' poetry, but rather a selection of poems by Christians of widely differing interests and experience. The variety of ideas, subjects and styles included reflects this diversity.

The compiler, Gordon Bailey, is a freelance writer and journalist and has had four books of his own poetry published. This compilation grew out of his contacts with Christian writers and his desire to put together a collection of poetry being written by Christians, by both established and unknown writers.

100 CONTEMPORARY CHRISTIAN POETS

Compiled by Gordon Bailey

A LION PAPERBACK
Tring · Belleville · Sydney

For works previously published, see 'Acknowledgements' on page 10

Published by
Lion Publishing plc
Icknield Way, Tring, Herts, England
ISBN 0 7459 1042 4
Lion Publishing Corporation
10885 Textile Road, Belleville, Michigan 48111, USA
ISBN 0 7459 1042 4
Albatross Books Pty Ltd
PO Box 320, Sutherland, NSW 2232, Australia
ISBN 0 86760 673 8

First edition 1983
Reprinted 1983
This edition 1985

Cover photograph by Lion Publishing: Jon Willcocks

Printed and bound in Great Britain by
Cox & Wyman Ltd, Reading

Contents

Introduction

Over the years I had read a great deal of poetry written by Christians, a proportion of which I felt was good and worth publishing. In fact, I realized that there was a wealth of unpublished talent and, as I came across many poets who had had their work published in magazines and periodicals, I became convinced that they deserved a much wider audience. So I decided to put together a collection of poetry being written by Christians, by both established and unknown writers.

After discussions at meetings of the Birmingham Arts Group, I wrote to every Christian publication I could think of to ask Christian writers to send me their poetry. The response was truly overwhelming, so much so that I had to ask two friends to help me read through the vast quantities of material which kept pouring in. Making the final selection was a difficult task.

So, here is the anthology. Is this 'Christian poetry'? A question which is bound to be asked. I don't believe there is such a thing as Christian poetry, any more than there are Christian verbs, adjectives or nouns. These are the poems, on a wide variety of topics and themes, of writers who are committed Christians. I hope that you will be aroused, challenged, amused, disturbed; that the poems I have chosen will affect for good your intellect, your emotions, your will. I offer this collection for your enjoyment, your pleasure and your contemplation.

Gordon Bailey

Acknowledgements

Thanks to Phil Thomson and Anthony Rose for their invaluable help in reading through the many thousands of poems to make this selection; to Nick Page and the production team of his Sunday morning BBC Radio 2 show who appealed to listeners to submit poems; and to the editors of many Christian newspapers and periodicals who gave free space, allowing us to request readers to submit poetry for consideration.

All poems are copyright and appear by permission of the authors. The following poems have been previously published and are included by kind permission of the copyright-holders:

Sir John Betjeman: 'Church of England', 'Harvest Hymn' and 'Matlock Bath' from *Collected Poems*, reprinted by permission of John Murray (Publishers) Ltd.

Jack Clemo: 'Whispers' and 'Broad Autumn' from *Broad Autumn*, and 'Eros in Exile' from *Cactus on Carmel*, by permission of Methuen London Ltd.

Keith Freeman: 'Devon Girl' and 'Remembrance Sunday' from *An Element of Time*, by permission of Downlander Publishing.

Michel Quoist: 'We Have too Much to do' and 'I want to be Somebody' from *Meet Christ and Live*! and 'All' from *Prayers of Life*, by permission of Gill and Macmillan Ltd.

Evangeline Paterson: 'And That Will Be Heaven' from *The Lion Book of Christian Poetry*, reprinted by permission of the author.

Dick Williams: 'Old Church' and 'Middle Age' from *Beyond Eden*, reprinted by permission of the author.

Susan Williams: 'The Bindweed and the Rose' from *Beyond Eden*, and 'Liverpool Cathedral' from *Portrait of a Diocese*, reprinted by permission of the author.

CAROLINE ACKROYD

For I am Meek and Lowly in Heart

Presumably as the only Son He could have chosen
Any gift, any means of persuasion.
He could have had beauty, forcing attention;
He could have been Mozart,
David the musician,
Singer of the psalms amid the tribal slaughter
Turned the harp gut to water, to a singing stream.
He could have been a sculptor
Carving the cedar
Gold-coating the creature
Achieved for the Temple, the temple splendour;
Or a poet
To send words forth like fishing boats
On the blue pages of the water.

But He chose none of these things
Leaving each gift for some other
And took for Himself healing, humanity;

Only God could be so proof against glamour.

This act of Divine humility,
Does it not make renunciation the true test
Of the revolutionary?

CAROLINE ACKROYD

December 25th

I am caught between the firelight and the dying sun
This short and burnished afternoon
This Christmas.
I am held in the path of the sun
Saint Paul on the road to Damascus.

In this personal artistic room
The Christmas tree in bloom
Gleams deep with man-made colour;
In pewter, like flowers of light,
Are white and yellow blossoms of the winter.

The steady flagrance of the sun is love
In this room
It is love burning
Limitless
Throughout the universe
We are held in its path.

With the night comes music
Drains into silence
And the aftermath.

SIMON ALEXANDER

Apocalyptic

If the snow fell in summer,
  Settled on the bee's neck,
  Clogging the dandelion clock,
  Freezing the fly in the swallow's beak,
If the heater and the numb-er
  Attacked simultaneously to cap all
  The embryos of the apple,
  The blossoming of the maple:
The wind would be like a strummer
  Not knowing which song –
  A summer chorale, or the long
  Hard solo of winter with its strong
Strident blasts, to sing. While the thunder
  Murmurs in distant strongholds,
  Knocks on the bedded cloud-tops, folds
  And unfolds its razored whites and golds,
Wagging electric elbows under
  Them, to ions assembled on peaks and spires,
  And swallows or starlings on the wires
  Swirled into flocks, and sparks from the fires
Rise among snowflakes as they wander
  This way, and that, drifting miliary
  Specks of cold and heat, flecked, till the
  Bright wings of the fritillary
Are lost in a dancing August dune:
  Is it the apocalyptic question?
  Are Melchizedek and Apollyon
  Let loose on the streets of Zion
De novo – as we assume
  Uncertain millenial cycles?
  Shall Satan's cosmic dream, or Michael's
  Poison the ancient stream that trickles
On to its accustomed stone?

CATHY ANDERSON

Love Song

I set the pattern of stars and sun
And while they remain
You are fixed in my mind

And the course of the fox and the rabbit
A lad and his lady
The way of a woman with child.

While the waves run onto the beach
And the whale ploughs his road through the ocean
My love reaches out.

As long as the deer runs his race;
Until you can measure the edges of space
I will keep you.

CATHY ANDERSON

Dying

A blind man is running on the beach;
The hot sun on his back and skull,
        thin as egg shell wakes him,
And he reaches a chicken arm
For a fag on the dresser where
        driftwood and pebbles rank
With boys in khaki and family –
Soon they will be laying
Arnold Noel Selbie
dead.

The light is tea-stained, one tendril of ivy
        locked about the window
Where he is in bed, his skin hard
        as nut, cold as ash on the pillow
And sucking another cigarette
        between feeds, fragile blue eyes watch
        his mother, who in all her misty dreaming,
Her wildest guess, never saw him barnacled,
His last voyage like this.

CORRINE BAILEY

I Want my World Back

I want my world back God.
Why did you let them take it away?
My world was large and colourful,
I knew it so well.
My world was filled with family and friends,
house and garden,
shops and church;
there were trees to see and flowers to smell,
there were wide blue skies and black rain clouds;
there were the pictures on the walls of my home;
dog-hairs on the carpets,
clothes in my wardrobe and washing on the line.
Where has it all gone Lord?
Please can I have it back?

Pain came and they said I had to leave my world
for a while.
My world was large and colourful, then:
a ride in an ambulance,
a red-brick building,
a long corridor,
and my world shrank to a large cream room
and a world of beds and strangers.

Lying on my back I can't see the flowers
or the trees
only a glimpse of sky if I turn my head.
There aren't any pictures on the walls
and I don't suppose they have a dog here either.
Lord,
I don't want a world where I can't see my friends
when I want to,
where I can't hold hands with my family
or complain about the ironing;
I feel trapped in this smaller world.
Lord, when will you let me out?

I used to walk in the garden
now I am not allowed to walk at all
not even among these strangers,
each one trapped, like me,
in a shrinking world of pain and pills.

Do they feel as I do?
I don't know.
I don't even think I care.
I can take my painkillers and tranquilizers
and my two sleeping tablets
and I don't have to think about their problems –
or mine.
Then my world would be only me.
I would be alone,
free from pain from worry from family from friends
and from strangers.
But – stop! Wait!
I could never be alone. . .
the Creator of the *whole* world is with me;
my world is his world and his world is mine.
How vast his world is,
how great he is.
What does he want of me
in this new world of mine?

He wants to open my eyes
to open me
to help me to see again
to feel again
to reach out and touch the lives of others.
Lord,
I understand now:
my world is not smaller but larger
because you have extended it.

Thank you Lord
for this opportunity
to laugh and cry
and hold the hands of strangers.

GORDON BAILEY

Regenesis One

In the beginning
of the days of re-creation,
the God of heaven, become the Man of earth,
(the life of mankind having become
formless, empty, and deep in darkness)
said: 'Let there be Light.'
And Light entered Jerusalem
carried by a mule,
and the Light was good.
The Light was called Jesus.
This was the first day.

And God said: 'Let the Light shine in the darkness.'
Jesus shone,
dispelling darkness, to begin with, from the temple,
illuminating the gloom of usury,
enlightening the place of worship with His glory.
He drew a distinction between darkness and Light,
and the Light was good.
This was the second day.

And God said, 'Let gifts be gathered into my treasury.'
A widow, with only two pennies to rub together,
gave all she possessed to God;
then, concerned by the smallness of her gift,
crept away in shame.
But Jesus pointed out that she had given God everything.
Not only did God see that this was good,
He was caused to remember that His Son was soon to
give everything.
This was the third day.

And God said, 'It will be necessary for me to die.'
And,
whilst Mary of Bethany anointed Him beforehand for burial,
Judas made arrangements to betray his Master.
And God saw the love of Mary and said:
'Let this be made known wherever the gospel is preached.'
This was the fourth day.

And God said: 'All life, at its very best, is summed up in my Son,
Jesus.'
And Jesus explained how He, as Life, would be made available,
to be shared by all mankind:
He took bread, gave thanks, broke it, blessed it, and said,
'This is my body, given for you;'
He took wine, poured it out, shared it with His followers, saying,
'This is my blood, shed for all of you.'
Through disloyalty, betrayal, and arrest,
the availability of eternal life for all was threatened,
but God looked upon His Son,
and was well pleased.
This was the fifth day.

And God remembered that
He had originally created mankind in His own image,
and now mankind was demanding the crucifixion of His Son.
And God saw the apostle Peter deny Christ profanely;
and God saw justice wiped away with a towel,
and the law mocked by those who claimed to cherish it most;

and God watched, with sorrow, the suicide of Judas;
and God saw a king abdicate his responsibility,
demeaning his kingship,
as, together with his servants,
he joined in the inhuman maltreatment of an innocent
prisoner;
and God saw His Son crucified,
then, suddenly, God found He could watch no more;
and the world was convinced it had seen its Light
extinguished.
And God saw those who had believed in the Light,
dark of mood, barren of hope,
bury the body of His Son.
God saw all that had been done;
and there was evening, and there was morning –
the sixth day.

On the seventh day
God and the whole universe
rested.

In the early hours of the morning of the next day,
Roman soldiers, seated in darkness,
were startled as, from within the dark interior of the
tomb,
Light shone, growing brighter,
surrounding them;
and Light gave life to their legs as they fled;
and Light dried Mary's tears,
and Light shone brilliantly into the hearts and minds
of the disciples, flooding their lives
with His indwelling presence.
And, for them,
it could be said,
this was the first day.

GORDON BAILEY

Spring

Clear the air and crisp the focus,
swarms of snowdrops, clumps of crocus;
melting snow cavorts and trickles
down the shiny holly's prickles.

Tall and statesmanlike this fellow:
suited green and hatted yellow,
faces frosts and charms the chill,
dapper daring daffodil.

New-born leaf the tree enhances,
heralding the Spring's advances;
gone the winter's stormy resting,
dunnock vies with wren for nesting.

Latter day outlives the former,
sun is higher, rain is warmer;
comes pale blossom to the prunus,
proof of resurrection newness.

GORDON BAILEY

It'll Never Catch On

Listen, I'm telling you,
it'll never catch on!
I'm the guy with the advertising agency,
you're the bloke with the boat, right?
You want a motif, a logo, a symbol for your set-up,
and you came to me
with this crazy idea;
listen, you said your set-up stands for
life, liberty, truth, love, joy, peace, hope,
all the big stuff;
well then, you'll have to have a symbol which
a lady will wear at her wrist or her throat,
or a gent will attach to the lapel of his coat;
what d'you mean: 'What's a lapel?'?
I mean, what set-up standing for life
is going to expect its members to wear a badge
with something totally inappropriate on it,
like a, er, a guillotine,
or a gas chamber,
or an electric chair,
or a gallows?
You gotta have a symbol that'll catch on,
a dove, an eagle,
spirit of life and freedom,
right?
Yeh, well, if that's how you feel.

Here, George,
I just had this chap come in,
belongs to this set-up,
you know, they stand for all the big ideals,
life, liberty, love, like that,
and he had this idea for a logo:
a cross!

Yeh, a cross!
Your actual means of execution.
Yeh – right!
I thought what sorta lady is gonna wear a cross round her neck!
That's right, exactly what I said:
it'll never catch on,
never in a thousand years!

JOHN BAMPTON

On Fame

Fame : Oh Exciting Queen we bend to thee
Thy child 'Ambition' drives us on
Blinded by starry light we fail to see
The crumbling edifice we build upon
We sacrifice to bask in thy beams
Life's glorious aeons and tender ties
Heaven lost to realise our dreams
And win a glance from thy fair eyes

SHEILA BARCLAY

High Hopes

I long to go, dancing, to eternity
to follow the snatched music that I hear
coming and going through my days.
But in my dreaming nights I dance –
I dance, enough to wear my slippers out.

And in that giant dance, the world's involved,
and wheels within wheels revolve around,
and hands go clapping,
hair streams gleaming out
and all is life and light and praise.

When can I go, feet springing
up and down, to everlasting joy?

SHEILA BARCLAY

Here's Looking at You

My eyes half blind with love
I see, flesh of my flesh,
your beauty and your flaws.
In you I see my faults and so
I spare them, then condemn,
then pity that your legacy's so poor.

Your humour and your courage
lift my heart high with pleasure
and with hope,

but there are times I long to have a lap
so wide, and breasts so big
that I could hide you from the hurt
of life's confusion.

Yet, I look on and let you go
to find out cruelty and pain.

I watch you grow, communicate,
and form your own life's values.
I see it all. I weep
with helplessness.

Yet I am here
and what I can, I give you.
That is all.

TODD BARNHART

Armistice

once there was a war
    no tanks,
    no missiles,
    no jets,
    no bayonets,
    no submarines,
    no infantry,
    no cavalry charges.
but –
everyone died
when war broke out
between you and me
and love lost.

RICHARD BAUCKHAM

Epithalamion

All our love is deeply (as a folk
tale in the memory of once upon
a time the golden-haired princess awoke
from spellbound slumbers to a carillon
of kisses) grounded in the depth of his
own dying. For the risk of love we dare
(the peasant boy with rustic pleasantries
courted the princess of the golden hair)
because the tale is told (how she was brought
a virgin victim to the dragon's lair,
a bride self-bartered for her people's weal)
of love as strong as death (our hero fought
with death's dark reptile) that our hearts may bear
his true love as an everlasting seal.

ROSEMARY BAZLEY

Espalier

A pear tree in my orchard stands
Against a sun-swept wall;
The gardener with his hoary hands
Has nailed it fast with iron bands
That it should never fall.

Now as I pass it beckons me
With branches pinioned wide;
And in those tortured arms I see
A fettered Figure on a Tree –
Creation crucified.

PATRICK BERTHOUD

It is Dark Now and a Warm Wind Blows

It is dark now and a warm wind blows,
Tossing the straggling hedge-tops
In a whirl of dark against a clammy grey.
Heads high we laugh along the road
And footstep sounds are ript
On to the destination of the wind
Before our ears accept the sound.

It is darker now; the warm wind spits
Stealing a dribbling spume of dew
From clouds which hang above unseen.
The spots are flecked upon our faces
Only to be breathed away
Above the road and out across the moor
Before our skins can feel the wet.

It is night now and we turn against the wind.
Our shouted thoughts snatched from our mouths,
Are tossed like bubbles on a wave of air.
Allusions to a play half-read,
A theory with nought but gaiety as evidence,
All these the warm wind banters in the dark
Behind our heads and out beyond our time.

SIR JOHN BETJEMAN

Church of England thoughts occasioned by hearing the bells of Magdalen Tower from the Botanic Garden, Oxford On St. Mary Magdalen's Day

I see the urn against the yew,
  The sunlit urn of sculptured stone,
I see its shapely shadow fall
On this enormous garden wall
  Which makes a kingdom of its own.

A grassy kingdom sweet to view
  With tiger lilies still in flower
And beds of umbelliferae
Ranged in Linnaean symmetry,
  All in the sound of Magdalen tower.

A multiplicity of bells,
  A changing cadence, rich and deep
Swing from those pinnacles high
To fill the trees and flood the sky
  And rock the sailing clouds to sleep.

A Church of England sound, it tells
  Of 'moderate' worship, God and State,
Where matins congregations go
Conservative and good and slow
  To elevations of the plate.

And loud through resin-scented chines
  And purple rhododendrons roll'd,
I hear the bells of Eucharist
From churches blue with incense mist
  Where reredoses twinkle gold.

Chapels-of-ease by railway lines
  And humble streets and smells of gas
I hear your plaintive ting-tangs call
From many a gabled western wall
  To Morning Prayer or Holy Mass.

In country churches old and pale
  I hear the changes smoothly rung
And watch the coloured sallies fly
From rugged hands to rafters high
  As round and back the bells are swung.

Before the spell begin to fail,
  Before the bells have lost their power,
Before the grassy kingdom fade
And Oxford traffic roar invade,
  I thank the bells of Magdalen Tower.

SIR JOHN BETJEMAN

Harvest Hymn

We spray the fields and scatter
  The poison on the ground
So that no wicked wild flowers
  Upon our farm be found.
We like whatever helps us
  To line our purse with pence;
The twenty-four-hour broiler-house
  And neat electric fence.

All concrete sheds around us
  And Jaguars in the yard,
The telly lounge and deep-freeze
  Are ours from working hard.

We fire the fields for harvest,
  The hedges swell the flame,
The oak trees and the cottages
  From which our fathers came.
We give no compensation,
  The earth is ours today,
And if we lose on arable,
  Then bungalows will pay.

All concrete sheds . . . etc.

SIR JOHN BETJEMAN

Matlock Bath

From Matlock Bath's half-timbered station
  I see the black dissenting spire –
Thin witness of a congregation,
  Stone emblem of a Handel choir;
In blest Bethesda's limpid pool
Comes treacling out of Sunday School.

By cool Siloam's shady rill –
  The sound are sweet as strawberry jam:
I raise mine eyes unto the Hill,
  The beetling HEIGHTS OF ABRAHAM;
The branchy trees are white with rime
In Matlock Bath this winter-time,

And from the whiteness, grey uprearing,
  Huge cliffs hang sunless ere they fall,
A tossed and stony ocean nearing
  The moment to o'erwhelm us all:
Eternal Father, strong to save,
How long wilt thou suspend the wave?

How long before the pleasant acres
  Of intersecting LOVERS' WALKS
Are rolled across by limestone breakers,
  Whole woodlands snapp'd like cabbage stalks?
O God, our help in ages past,
How long will SPEEDWELL CAVERN last?

In this dark dale I hear the thunder
  Of houses folding with the shocks,
The GRAND PAVILION buckling under
  The weight of the ROMANTIC ROCKS,
The hardest Blue John ash-trays seem
To melt away in thermal steam.

Deep in their Nonconformist setting
  The shivering children wait their doom –
The father's whip, the mother's petting
  In many a coffee-coloured room;
And attic bedrooms shriek with fright,
For dread of *Pilgrims of the Night*.

Perhaps it's this that makes me shiver
  As I ascend the slippery path
High, high above the sliding river
  And terraces of Matlock Bath:
A sense of doom, a dread to see
The *Rock of Ages cleft for me*.

JOAN A. BIDWELL

Supper Being Ended

In the quiet place
at close of day
he washes the feet of my mind from the dust of its fret.

His infinite eyes
see the staining and wounds of the road, his hands
bring smarting
and cleansing
and balm.

The grace of his health
restores my soul
her place in the circling stars of perpetual praise.

Then, taking again the seamless robe, the Alpha-Omega,
Master and Lord,
we talk together,
friend with friend.

LYNETTE BISHOP

First Sight

When was it
that we first glimpsed God?
Was it in the
red, wrinkled smallness
in the half light?
Or later in the strong feet
striding across hills
which a few aeons ago
he had called into being?
Or with a strange thrill
in the hand which
reached out to touch some
indescribable deformity
and make it whole?
Or in a sudden contact
with those searching eyes,
splitting men's hearts like pea-pods
to pour in?
Or was it yesterday
when in a moment
of forgetfulness
we lost ourselves
and came across him
unexpectedly
everywhere?

CATHERINE BONYE

The Partnership

He stood before me with his hand outstretched,
I was uncertain, kept mine back at first,
Not knowing what to say or what to do,
Whether to take his hand or linger on,
Where pale confusion hung like autumn mist,
And every day would end in tragedy.

I was the first to speak. He answered me
In gentle tones, as echoes of the wind
Sends shivers down the spines of many a man,
So did his voice to me, and as he spoke
My body seemed to tingle, wanting more,
As if this man alone could give my fill.

'My feet are so unsteady' 'Mine are strong.
I will support you long before you fall'
'My ways are lonely' 'But they need not be,
And I will give companions on your way'
'My eyes are dim' 'Then let me be your sight,
And you will find a clearer vision then'

'I often come to darkness' 'I am Light.
But trust me and you'll never see't again'
'And evil falsehoods' 'So I am the Truth,
And you need never fear while you have me'
'I know not where I'm going' 'I'm the Way.
Come, take my hand and trust me silently'

I put my hand in his, and from that point
My pressing troubles seemed so far away
That when I turned around I could not see
How such a small load had once weighed so much.
He kept my hand in his, and keeps it still,
And from that time we walked on together.

DAVID BOYD

Under my Feet, the Years Bide Time

I have come briefly
to be something other than a stranger
in this bleak unpeopled place
where once grain bare
cleft wood
was fitted handily length to length
and peat cover opened
for the apples of the earth.
Here on this furrowed face
long left
lazy bed
I will lay
me down
and watch
a million masts
running with the wind
smoke across the earth.

DAVID BOYD

Glendalough

St Kevin came
building stones
upon   stones
shaping earth
drinking water
praying with fire

And men of books came
with hearts and hands
and minds
and souls
city of God
sanctuary of thousands
for a time
and a season

And men of iron and steel came
and rent the veil
and spilt the water
and the blood
and darked the sky
so that men may no longer come in.

Still   Stones   Stand
in the glen
and the sky sometimes lies dark
above the lough
Now no soft footprints
but paths indelible
and for our pleasure men still steal silver
and the earth no longer trembles by St Kevin's
        penitential bed.

FRANK BUCHANAN

Golgotha: the Tree and the Hill

No dionysian tree
Earth rooted, vicious with cruelty
Of a rising sap;
No lopped branch with green jealousy
In each proud bud.
The tree is dead: pier prop
Out of sea mud,
Limber derelict, rafter
Crumbling to dust,
Sleeper slumped in the red
of its holed rust.

No temple grove
Groomed among trees; no shadow
Of hate-love images
In wood or stone;
No rhythmic ring space.
The hill is balder than the public pate
of black race,
White, brown, yellow: everyman place
Of a skull shored up. It's hell's enclave
Amorphous, dry, graveless as
Adam's grave.

VALERIE BUDD

Poem for Christmas

When I was young I built my life
On dreams, and on the hint of love
But as I grew, I chose new paths
Of darkness and uncertainty
I left the light
And chose to search for purpose and reality
The way grew darker step by step
Until at last I could no longer see to seek.

Lost and tired I longed for the dreams,
For the love of my youth –
But the door of the inn was closed,
                    I stopped.
Sank down in the mire of my own travelling
In the dust of my shattered hopes.
Kneeling alone, trembling,
          and so desperately afraid
My life in ashes, my spirit broken
At last I know why I need you, Lord.

I come to You empty handed
I come to You blinded by darkness
I come for You to fill me with Your life
And with Your light that showed
Wise men the way
Your light that even shepherds understood

Oh Saviour, thank you for the love
That's willing to be born, even in such
A stable as this my heart.

DOROTHY BULL

Prospects of Glory

(John 17:22–24)

See the perfection of a single rose –
Then multiply it by each flower that grows:
Wonder upon the texture of its bloom,
Beauty of colour, form, and sweet perfume,
On earth behold its glory!

From lofty height gaze on a cloudless day
Upon a scene to take your breath away:
The awesome grandeur of the mountain peak,
The shining ribbon of the river's creek,
On earth behold their glory!

The colours of the sunset sky behold –
Pale turquoise streaked with roseate hues, or gold;
Clouds, silver-lined; star-studded skies at night;
The smiling radiance of the moon's strange light;
Above behold their glory!

But how much greater will the prospect be
For Christians who behold the heavenly!
The Saviour willed, in His High-Priestly prayer
That such should His eternal kingdom share,
And there behold His glory!

Before He had the world's foundation laid
God's love was in His only Son displayed,
And that same love extends to all mankind,
Oh, what amazing grace, when eyes, once blind,
Behold His perfect glory!

RAYMOND CHAPMAN

Intimations

Henry Vaughan saw eternity
and far beyond star countries;
Blake met angels in the garden
pleasantly building green Jerusalem.

I border bred, London extended,
little matchstick man
for whom the sparrows do not care two farthings,
remain untutored by exceptions

Lord keep us in our proper stations.

If the communion of saints
is not only the shining ones
but the incompetent and ineffective,
let grace sidle down the repeated street
and a wing flash in ambiguous sunlight.

RAYMOND CHAPMAN

Jonah

When he came racing up the beach
    with a dead man's beard on his chin

Mad Moll shrieked like an owl
    and the children ran,
    houses melted into mud
    red bats flew out of the sun
    trees split like a beggar's shirt

it was, I remember, a good year for gourds

Some said they saw the fish
    larking away offshore
but most reckoned it another stunt –
eat more – drink more – pay more –
    till the big boss took it hard:
    we too, in the end.

The town's not much better now;
    life went on after he sailed away
    but with a sort of difference

something different

a fellow who goes under for three days
and charges back to tell you there's still time.

RAYMOND CHAPMAN

House Communion

Here on this accustomed table
    dull stained by family meals
    and spilled milk of past infancy,
    elbowed in friends' fellowship,

as my own house-guest I break bread,
    hosted by heart's depth,
    charged with mimetic obedience
    offer what is not my own.

May the presence hold on hasty mornings
    and through evenings of weariness
    justifying the repetitions
    of all failures that venture on worthiness.

PETYA CHRISTIE

'Was That my Gethsemane Hour?'

Was that my Gethsemane hour,
As I agonized in confusion of thought?
Or my abandonment upon the cross
When thought itself seemed dead?
Was it not rather I who know Him not?
Or hastened up a hill to hurl this wretched body
From a gallows tree of my own making,
Of my disbelief?
There is no certainty but this –
He caught me as I fell.

PETYA CHRISTIE

Walk of Witness

Budding trees snow-laden.
Beautiful the paradox –
The dying Christ has risen.

Sun-fused snow-tears falling.
Hardened though my heart be,
Melts at His touch.

JACK CLEMO

Whispers

These whispers must come from ahead,
From a point where the road bends round
Into faith-flushed terrain again,
Beyond the last factory-shed
of secular mirage. They have haunted
Not merely my raw birth-dower
Of iron tracks, quarry faces
And thin sand-scratching furze,
But palm and pebbly beach more fitly hers
Whose whisper warms, confirms their message.

To tire of current babble
Could not evoke such clear intimations
Unless something lived and moved, articulate
Outside the jarring circuit: without this,
My fret or boredom could bring only
The screwed frost of silence.

I am not tired: the whispers give me power,
Not insulating, sealing me in an archaic climate.
I have trudged the menaced and changeful way
Down through the twentieth century,
Smelt petrol, drugs and bleaching chemicals,
Passed supermarkets, laboratories, clinics.

I have heard men's voices barking on the moon,
Bomb-clouts and the shrieked pop tune;
Stood under excavators that baptized me
With rain from their poised dull teeth;
Seen white spoil-heaps, first conical, turn oblong,
And subtler crusts of thought turn sour.

I know what today's paper claims
For the birth-pill, what some bishops preach
About a shrivelled God and shrivelling morals,
And what young trendy poets write
Concerning urinals.
I have caught the dry jargon, watched the expert hands
Plaster neat labels on holy places,
Call the terrible secret of God a neurosis,
The terrible insights of sex an obsession.

The whispers that echo in my lines
Laugh gently among buds of the future,
For a wind will rise against the vulgar term,
And terror is truth in the intermediate
Regions between nullity and centre.

If flawed cells flared in the murmuring germ
Till I rasped and hurled rocks like a clay titan,
There is no regret on the lulled levels,
For they are private. The rebel's
Fire and peril remain; intense
Listening stiffens my rejection
Of the broad escape-route's signs.
Even her pebbly beach under the calm bran-
Coloured cliff borders the colite quarries
Where stone was cracked to bear
A whispering gallery, like our faith's, ringed by
 nightmare.

JACK CLEMO

Eros in Exile

Locked grove, lost grove.
Heavy air from mouldering clay-hills
Fills the arbour and threatens the embrace.
Nuptial bud at the lips
Slips back into the natural stream
Which gyrates blindly in the tense wood,
Offering no drink, taking no reflections:
Opaque dull gloss of instinctive waters
Suddenly untransmuted. Male tower, female flower,
Cower in the grey light. Pride of the copse
Drops as the timid hazel-stems
Lift from the thickened brook their soiled catkins.

Errs flesh or soul that the sense of an intruder
Has renewed some primordial guilt,
Turning bride-bank to silt?
Itch and urge, pitch and surge,
Flatten to a confused cry
Now to conceal, now to defy.
Smeared wings flutter but cannot fly
After the fierce dip that evades true contact.

Foiled bud and wing, soiled catkins – and above,
Outside, wooden beams crossed on the clay-hill.
Another cry, a tie with another temple
More deeply penetrating:
By the rivers of Babylon
We lay down but could not love.

Text from the clear springs, the erect tower,
The surging stem:
If I forget thee, O Jerusalem,
Let my right hand forget her cunning,
Let my right hand forget,
Feel only the deadened stream, dead dream.

So we have but lapsed, in truancy,
Just for a moment, to this drab
Stab of morality.

JACK CLEMO

Broad Autumn

True faith matures without discarding.
All I unearthed, each sky-sign crudely mapped
On the white rasped hills of youth,
Warms me still by rowan-tapped crags,
Far up the autumnal mountain,
Incredibly remote in climate, texture, weathering
Of bare stones, from my first insights:
I leave no wreckage on those low rasped cones.

There is no snarl of tools
Where broad wisdom calls across the cordial heather,
But the hacked glints my young heart stored
Still tone the subtle comforts and the sharp
Fearful shifts of shade as the blood cools
To admit, and clarify, the expanding mental range.

No pestilence of proud ripeness,
Urbane, agnostic, cankers the wide braes
Which my spirit, eagle-keen now, calls native
In the pale sun's gloss. The spikes of raw praise,
Sparse once on the white hills,
Glow ruddier here against the thinned
Thieving of the schooled foreign crows.

I have not changed my country; I have grown and
explored
In my faith's undivided world.
I discard no primal certainty, no rasped
Sky-sign of the Cross;
But now in broad autumn, feeling a new peace
And the old poise of defence,
I accept the pure trysting lochs,
The full antler in the glens.

JIM DONNELLY

The God for Everyman

I am the spirit of the air,
I am the wanderer who roams,
I am the cloud of unknowing,
I am the water that purifies.
I am the face of all things good,
I am the star that guides at night,
I am the dove of peaceful skies,
I am the heart which stirs all life.
I am the king of every king,
I am the sun to warm the earth,
I am the lover of the pure,
I am the judge where justice reigns.
I am the earth to live upon,
I am the God for everyman.

MICHAEL J. DOUGLAS

Field Flower

I hold it in my hands, and see
Frail marvel of Divinity.

For this: fresh winds of morning blew,
And meadows fed night-long on dew.

Or some June songbird pleaded rain
To ease the brown earth's fevered pain.

Came dawn, and under summer skies
A wonder feast to hold my eyes.

For fairest heaven wooed earth, to place
Its seal of beauty on her face.

So delicately rare, so fine –
This perfect thought of God is mine!

I hold it in my hands, and see
Frail marvel of Divinity.

JOHN DUTTON

Out of Reach

Reaching – I can't reach far enough.
So someone stretched out a hand.
And someone put a nail in it.

JOHN DUTTON

Careful of Me

Treading cautiously,
in case I step upon a toe or two.
Afraid to offend
          anyone who happens to be there.

Holding hands tenderly,
in case I fail to touch a heart or two.
Eager to attend
          anyone who happens to be there.

Always looking out for people.
Afraid to miss them; in case they miss me.

SUE ELKINS

Bedsit

Seated
By the one-bar electric fire
In the one room
Someone else somehow calls home
    (the grease-stain from a badly-packed
    take-away chow mein
    spreading on the knee of my jeans,
    rock music spilling into the unwarmed air
    from a transistor radio on the floor)
I'm drinking coffee.
Always drinking coffee.

And in how many rooms
Around the fringes of the capital
Do other girls eat mock-Chinese food,
And, coffee-drugged,
Sit up late on floor cushions,
Discussing what he said last night
    and how they lost a pound by missing lunch three
        days last week
    and how they'd look without a fringe,
And, having talked their hearts away,
Walk, haloed by the street-lights,
Back to their own one-room world,
Looking to the next night's conviviality
To take away the pain
Of the never-ending
Search for something more?

BARRY ETHERIDGE

Communication

'The daffodils are nice again.'
She paused at the window
Expecting no reply
And he in his armchair sat
Reading F.T. as if understood
Until, puzzled by the crossword,
He snatched his slippers from the dog,
A black and white spaniel with quizzical eyes
Long puzzled by cross words and empty silence.
Crossing the floor with painful step
He paused before the window
Where, as if stricken by the beauty of the toil,
He breathed deeply and,
Sighing,
Proclaimed,
'The daffodils are nice again.'

BARRY ETHERIDGE

Vietnam

We came as an army
Choked on winter song and baked bean breakfast,
Straight lined.

We came to see the conquered,
Kill to kill the killing;
Tortured humanity discarded
And left to mop the blood.

On orders we murder,
Of ourselves revolt and tear to shreds;
All faceless.
'Enemy!', scream
And run to find escape.

Some boast of wounds.
Others, faint with terror,
Kill for freedom,
All, with one heart,
Seek home.

And the lucky few,
If luck has teeth in this devil's mouth,
Will return,
With broken limbs or ravaged minds.

But here, in the face of death,
Lay only napalm flowers on the grave
And let us not remember
That once he had a name
For to carry Hell's reminder
Would infect the very healing
That we were sent to bring.

Senseless weapon against senseless body,
We flog a dead horse for revenge.

And many deal Death the victor's hand
Long before the whitened eyes ever stare
On naked fear.
We do not know to what they flee.
They have not fought for long enough
To learn, as we have learned,
That there is nowhere
That man can rest in peace.

PETER FENWICK

A Girl – to her Soldier Lover

David, do you remember as I do
  Long nights of summer, when the soft, warm air
Whispered among the birchwoods and we two
  Wandered the lanes of Kent? A happy pair
We were, and saw the crescent moon
  Fling silver magic from the dreaming sky
And never thought to lose it all so soon –
  The one to live alone, the one to die.

David, do you remember as you lie
  In that far grave, which I shall never see,
How once a single word, a single sigh
  Could wake to golden flame your love for me?
How then it seemed a sudden melting fire
  Welded your lips to mine and breast to breast
Joy in ecstatic striving of desire
  We found and in love's consummation rest.

Now all is ended and the empty years
  Stretch on before me like an endless way
Leading nowhere, and my bitter tears
  Can find no comfort. Some have bid me pray
And talked to me of God and mocked my grief
  With tales of Providence and will not see
One thought alone could bring my heart relief –
  David, that you remember me.

PETER FENWICK

A Soldier to the Christians

To you, who have not felt or seen as I
The bitter irony of lovely things,
Who think to find salvation in the sky
And ride to heaven on an angel's wings –

To you I leave the flowers and birds and trees
(You have not seen the blood or felt the pain)
To you the mighty mountains and the seas,
The waters' music and the touch of rain
(The love of beauty stirs your hearts to tears
Who could not weep when we marched out to slay)
To you the rosary of futile years,
The superstitious chain of night and day.

Myself, I loved life too and loved to rise
In exultation on the wings of youth,
But those same wings in breaking made me wise
And with the blood of men I purchased truth.

Therefore I leave to you, who cannot see,
This mockery called life and for my part
Rejoice that I shall quickly cease to be,
That nothingness shall still my foolish heart.

I ask no honour, neither do I crave
The empty praise of those who bade me kill –
Only the sweet oblivion of the grave
Where birds no longer sing, where all is still.

PETER FIRTH

'In my City'

In my city
There are clean roads
And kind trees watching the streets.
There are old buildings
Rooted in time,
And new shops
To sell me life.
In my city
There are cafés and friends,
There are doctors and schools,
And an iron bridge
As old as iron bridges are;
And every summer
A circus and a fair
Decorate the high green acres
North of Blackboy Hill,
And music, money and laughter
Tinkle into the night
Under a thousand coloured lamps.

Yet only days ago in my city
The night was aflame with burning cars,
And hatred ran down our back
Streets like a cold finger;
Men shook their injustices like fists,
And their voices were flying stones.
We never thought that this could happen here;
We thought that all was well.

But all is not well
When three boys meet one job,
And only the unemployment clerk
Knows your name,
And law seems to have the purpose
Of depriving you of dignity.

Yet those cries for help
Remind me
That violence is the voice
Of those to whom no-one has listened . . .

Lord,
I shall meet people today
Whose lives have not worked out
As they planned/desired.
Help me to listen
For what lies behind their frowns
And suspicion, and even their silence.

I take so many good things for granted
And assume that all is well with everyone else.
Today,
My listening could help one voiceless person
To state a case,
Cry a frustration,
Tell reality as they suffer it.

In my own times of need
Others have listened;
And when they responded,
It was Your voice that I heard:
That is Your way with us.
In my city, my street, my house,
Are those who feel by-passed by the world.
And through my listening,
Perhaps hope could separate them
From the violence of despair.
And since it *is* Your way with us,
It will be Your voice that they will hear.

PETER FIRTH

'Under the Earth'

Under the earth
On which we live
Lies the rock of the world –
Sandstone, limestone, chalk and granite –
The names ring like memories
Of school.
And we have chosen rock
As symbol of that which lasts –
Rock-like, we say; firm as a rock
And built on a rock.
Yet the rains of time
Reduce the hills to sand,
And great mountains in the end
Serve to feed river-beds.
The certain mountains,
Like the certain gods of old,
Pass into history.

And faith, built on a rock,
Trembles and looks back to firmer days,
And longs for the solidity of stone,
And hymns of childhood
And the fixed point of heaven.

But if God is like a river,
Constant, but always on the move,
if he is transparent as wind
or clean as rain,
Then the passing of mountains
And all dissolving rocks
Are evidence of life,
Movements of renewal,
As he moves on.

Lord, I do so long for certainties
And things that last.
Yet I would sooner know
That you are moving with me
On a journey,
Than growing smaller
Like the frozen memory of Sunday School.
You are a fast God,
always flowing.
I must be ready for the changes
You Yourself provide –
Changes of family and work,
Of age and understanding.
It is You,
Not time,
That is the flowing stream.

And if sometimes You are ahead of me,
Preparing places,
I will trust You to provide
The things I shall need there
When I arrive –
Strength to survive,
Jokes and friends to enjoy,
The vision to recognise signs of Your presence,
And the wisdom to move on
When you call.

THOMAS FOY

Thoughts at Christmas

Judea's hills are cold, and bleak, and rugged;
Judea's roads are rough this winter night
Judea's inns are full to overflowing –
What care these rich for poor men's sorry plight?

And so a cave is shelter for a Baby.
And here was born the Christ, that men might know
The depth of love that God has for His children,
Be hearts as black as night or white as snow.

Above that Babe a wooden cross is hanging;
Above that maiden-mother there sways a sword –
You took that sword and plunged it through her bosom;
I nailed upon that cross my Sov'reign Lord.

And every year, as dawns each Christmas Morning,
I pray the self-same prayer to Him Who died
On that dread cross that my hands coldly fashioned –
God, God, forgive us all this Christmastide.

KEITH FREEMAN

Devon Girl

Once you were not of the city.
The fields of concrete
surrounding you now,
Are not moved
By the wind of your thoughts
Drifting over them.
Their grey crops do not glint
In the light of a fading sun
Giving up the unequal struggle with the clouds,
After fighting to survive longer
In late afternoon.
Yet you have learned
That certain traits of people
Are indiscernible,
Like footsteps in a fog . . .

Lifting the suitcase, you pause
To shut the door,
Which hid so many scenes
Enacted without direction.
Your paths divide,
Perhaps something will provide
A rekindling of your affection.
But as you turn your gaze
Back to the room,
You see even the memories
Leaving.

KEITH FREEMAN

Remembrance Sunday

As the bell tolled and vibrated
It was though the dead were listening.
In those two minutes;
Was this the total time it took
For the millions dead in two world wars,
Actually to die –
The cumulative total of their dying seconds
Adds up to what?
Two minutes – a minute for each war?
Two minutes silence in a day where elsewhere
The guns still chatter to solve petty squabbles,
Where bombs fragment more than dreams,
Where some people don't need a knife
When they have a cudgel for a tongue,
Where eyes appear open
But hands are closed – tight.
Two minutes silence, and hard though I tried,
I couldn't hear a trumpet call from Heaven,
But felt the eyes of a father
Upon his children, watching their growth,
And maybe just sometimes wondering
Whether the death of his only son
Was really appreciated or understood,
Among so many deaths,
Among so many deaths . . .

JOHN GIBBS

Lazarus

I hate you, with your sores that you trade for charity,
Your leer, your fangs bared against intruders on your
    patch,
Your practised stories and your wheedling intonation.

Why do you hook onto me for Christ's sake?
I'm no Dives.
Where is my fine raiment?
When did I fare sumptuously?

But you know, and I know, that the world's awry.
My covenant to Oxfam makes no bridge
From Haves to Have Nots.
You'll stick around, like the tick on the ox,
Host and Parasite, you slob.

I cannot see you wafted to Abraham's bosom –
No bosom could stand you for long.
And for me there's no eternal damnation –
Its says nothing to me.
Our punishment is in the moment, when you ring.

CLARE GIRLING

Oxford June

I walked the summer streets of Oxford town
Bemused, while towers and trees patterned the sun
Shining through History, whose motes astir
Settled on serried stone. From alleys down,
Green ways led cool between grey walls. Upon
This grateful mat my feet sank soft; the whirr
Of shimmering insects soothed. As there I stood
On that rebounding turf, I saw aeons
Of life preserved. Trefoils in multitude,
Self-heal, eyebright, all flowers from ley and wood
Hid small in tiny camouflage, whose scions
Sprang from those ancient roots: a faery brood.
No sculptured spires surpass, nor learnings spoil,
These wondering blossoms welded to our soil.

CLARE GIRLING

The Pear Tree

The weathered pear, four generations old
My window-meditation, lives in peace.
Rough boughs, pale clouds of fragile blossom hold
Where slim bees hover. Tender leaves increase,
Light-fringed, to cup the summer sky and move
In gentle lifting through blue-dappled shade.
So may I ponder on such kindly Love
Which keeps in beauty every shining blade
Destined so soon to drift through Autumn air
Towards Winter dissolution: Glory lost
Reveals new grandeur of trimmed branches, bare
To the gale's strength, crisp outlined in chaste frost.
So wondering, I dream through the tree's year
Learning acceptance of God's Order here.

MARY GOODEY

The Keyboard Poet

Across vast space,
In the twinkling of a star,
The Eternal Spirit communicates
And is known.
Write the truth on these notes!
Let the keys speak in full dynamic range,
And through the keys, my fingers, nerves, heart,
Let unconsidered truth find expression,
Comprehension, acceptance.
Let me hold fast the message,
Iterate and reiterate,
Display it, set it in ivory,
Unfold it, bond, impart, celebrate, cradle,
Offer it up.

LUCY M. GREEN

Looking at Things

Wonder awoke in me
When, a child, I discovered feathers,
Marvelling at their softness, their delicacy of outline,
But still more at the sheen and ripple
Of changing colour, blue, and green and gold,
Gleaming across the peacock feathers I found –
Not the great eye-feathers only,
But tiny ones catching the light, to change as I turned them;
Yet never could all the colours be caught together.
The magic was in the moment, the glimpsing,
The passing enchantment,
Sweeter perhaps for the very swiftness of loss.

Shells with their circles of pearl
And hollowed, satin-smooth curves
Had their transient rainbows for my delight,
Shadows of rose and blue and pale sea-green;
Even the milky moonstones
Took on soft colours, like the ring of haze round the moon.
Mystery held them, as the colours were glimpsed, and then vanished.
I treasured the pearly shells, and the feathers,
Even as later in life I found joy
In the blue or gold fire of opals, caught for a moment;
Still more in the rainbow mist
Of a great waterfall, seen from afar,
Incredibly distant along a Norwegian valley;
Or the colours mingling in the flung spray of a wave.

It is given to us to see only one aspect in the moment,
One facet of the prism,
One colour of the spectrum;
That is enough of joy, but also enough of blindness
To bring humility, and kindle in us faith
That one day we may see life in its fulness
In the constant light of eternity;
Then may we know the whole of love blended in beauty,
Even as here on earth we see, for a passing moment only,
The rainbow with every colour alight in joy.

ANGELA GRIFFITHS

Echoes

It comes as no surprise to hear Him speak
When the ocean breakers roar,
Or when the breeze plays in the sycamores,
Or when the stormy night growls.
But,
When I hear Him in the hubbub of the city,
Where distant relatives turn a deaf ear
And dance to a tune of anarchy,
Then I cannot help but thank Him for the unexpected word.
And a prayer within me rises up
Until it meets and mingles with my risen Lord.

SALLY F. HARVEY

Anatomy of a Landscape

Feeding my wheels on the icy roadway,
the tortuous artery to the hills:
Life comes pumping along it from the heart of the
Brynamman
to fill the lanes, like capillaries networking the
mountainside
and petering out into cattlegrids and cottages;
And the air is different upon these heights,
born from a brilliant blue canopy's union with winter,
it hangs in frozen breezes,
chills the cheeks with breathtaking fingers;
The flocks, in pathetic bleatings,
demonstrate that the pulse, though feeble, is still beating –
they appear among the bones of the earth as grey as
boulders,
or as barnacles clinging to the slopes,
and chew miserably on frosted grass;
Meanderingly I paint flesh upon this rugged
skeleton:
in colours of green, bleached by sunshine,
that invariably miss the town below;
or in murky rainpools where the sky spilled over,
pierced by the highest peak;
I come for conversations with the cliffs,
but they keep their thoughts for heaven and receive no
replies,
only feathers blown over from winging birds
that drop like isolated hailstones onto the scenery;
And the promise I cling to
is of a fulness of view conceived in the crags
and brought forth from the windy precipice:
and spreadeagled below,
as the curtain of the sky unfolds to display its
offspring,
like the butterfly emerging from its obsolescent pupa,
newly washed, and worth waiting for.

STEWART HENDERSON

The Last Enemy

And He who each day
reveals a new masterpiece of sky
and whose joy
can be seen in the eyelash of a child
Who when He hears of our smug indifference
will whisper an ocean into lashing fury
and talk tigers into padding roars
This my God
whose breath is in the wings of eagles
whose power is etched in the crags of mountains
It is He whom I will meet
in whose presence I will find tulips and clouds,
kneeling martyrs and trees
The whole vast praising of His endless creation
And He will grant the uniqueness
that eluded me
in my earthly bartering with Satan
That day when He will erase the painful gasps of my ego
and I will sink my face into the wonder of His glorylove
and I will watch planets converse with sparrows
On that day
when death is finally dead

STEWART HENDERSON

Madeline

Madeline are you tired of the jokes,
The knock knock who's there
lesbian lesbian who lesbeavinyou.
Don't worry Madeline,
they're usually told by people frightened
of their own sexuality.
I've given up counting your tears Madeline.
Your eyes confused and unsure,
Your face preparing itself for despair.
Your heart full of empty passion and dreary rooms,
Your heart like a nervous sparrow fearing winter
You have considered death but found it too severe,
and life is now an endless sad humming.
Madeline come back from the past,
retreat from that bruised childhood.
Madeline come out of the closet
and go to your true lover.
Go to him Madeline
He's waiting for you,
The candles are lit,
an angel tasted the wine and went off dancing.
Go to him Madeline
your healing is in him,
go and be a woman for the Son of Man.

LYNDA HINGLEY

Easter

Early morning light and freshness
fills my eyes with shape and colour,
defines each leaf and blade of grass,
shimmers in each rainbow prism
which the breeze has gently shaken free . . .
    And darkness covers the earth.

Light and shade and life
reaching to the sun and air;
ducks scurrying, busy, dipping;
the wind in my hair, the coolness on my face;
the exultancy of movement, health and being . . .
    And my Lord hangs on a cross in death.

Cobwebs span the hedge
spaced with shining stars
spiralling in measured wholeness.
A proud swan circles in its own reflection
as the ripples spread and lap the stones . . .
    A broken body stiffens in a tomb.

Peace and quiet and stillness:
and a blackbird sings,
touches the sadness in my soul
and fills my eyes with tears of praise,
separate, yet shared in each and shared in One.
    Christ is risen! He is risen indeed!

PERCY HODGES

Companion

I shall not tread again the thymy sward
Whose springy roots leased footprints' dimples
For a brief second, but to erase them.
Or walk with her through heathery wastes
Where bleak stone walls tight-laced the tough green
fields,
Peeping a swirling sea whose flying spray
Silvery and rainbow-shot misted the scene.

I shall not hear again her voice
Eager to win my mind with slowing words.
She'd bend her head to hear intently, then
With dexterous phrase or sudden leap of thought
That reeled imagination to its bower,
Make music echo in the ceiling beams;
Or let her, laughing, lead me out
To where a pensive robin perched,
And all alone with crystalline notes
Practised its winter song.

I fortify my mind with memories
And when I ponder, sad, alone,
Where the soft twilight vaporous and silvery
Invades the room and creeps about
Dissolving the dark corners into mystery,
I sense her form and face
Etched in with shadows.
Then as I peer across the bay
She shows me where the waves
Wear creamy ripples flecked with gold.

MICHAEL HODGETTS

Verbum

It is a hollow trick
  Of poets to rehearse
  Despair in published verse.
The cardboard rhetoric
  Is governed half the time
  By fashion, or by rhyme.

Hamlet may doubt, Lear rage,
  But all the poet's art
  Is a performer's part
Remembered from the page.
  How can a greasepaint smear
  Express such doubt or fear?

Here in this altar-piece
  God hangs in agony
  Against a hellish sky:
And here pretence must cease?
  Not even here: the game
  Stops at the gilded frame.

The utterance defines:
  That measure of control
  Eases the tortured soul,
Breaks the beleaguered lines.
  So the Incarnate Word
  Hung silent and unheard.

TREVOR HOGGARD

The Storm

Rods of rain piledrive mercilessly into the tarmac
and bounce back
to the billowing, black clouds above;
the drains spew back the gurgling torrent's flow,
sweeping away bedraggled, drowning rats below.

Rrrrrrumble . . . CRACK! The heavens tear themselves
asunder;
buffeted pilots helplessly curse the thunder.
Lightning sizzles, the air's alight.
The moped driver anxiously looks for cover;
frightened children run to their frightened mother.

In agony radios hiss and spit;
a splintering tree screams as it is hit;
rain trickles from my squelching boots;
pea-pullers scatter to escape the carnage,
as God puts proud Man back into the Dark Age.

The digger's arm stretches imploringly towards the sky
but the arm of the cloud passes remorselessly by,
gradually disappearing over the hill;
the abandoned digger ruefully drips, weak and forlorn,
and thankful birds emerge to greet the second dawn.

NESTA M. HOWARD

The Trinity

The ox and ass, with unreflective gaze,
Sent steamy breath into the stable's cold;
God's crowning radiance broke to coloured rays
And their Creator stirred a memory old.
  So gladly they in recognition bowed
  Of Him who set the rainbow in the cloud.

The shepherds knew the songs that David sang –
That shepherd-boy anointed very king –
And so, when all the starry splendour rang
With songs of joy and words of counselling,
  They knew the swaddled Babe and Father one –
  God's life in man so humbly here begun.

But only Mary, since the angel came,
Had thoughts of Abram's knife and Hannah's vow,
Had proudly felt the piercing sword of shame
That she her Son could never hold or know.
  Yet by His Spirit, from the Father, He
  Was hers in all His single Trinity.

SUE HUDSPITH

Is This Me?

Who am I? What am I?
What makes me what I am?
The me you see, is it really me?
Or is it the me you want me to be?
Is it me as I am now?
Was yesterday's a different me
From the me I'll be tomorrow?

When you look at me, can you see
Everything that has happened to me?
Events, exchanges, and emotions
That fill every moment of every day,
Are added to me,
And make me the me that I am now.
But tomorrow's me will be different.

If a surgeon opened up my brain,
Could He see
The wealth of memory hidden there?
Hidden treasure, stored forever,
Hidden from him,
Hidden from you,
And mostly hidden from me, too.

Only God knows who I really am,
And every ingredient of the past
Which mixes up to make me me.
Only God knows the measures
Of each experience, strong and weak,
How they have affected me,
And what part of me they constitute.

And knowing all He loves me still.
And thinks me worth dying for.
And living once again in me,
The me I am,
Changes and alters the me I am,
And makes me more like Him.

LORNA INMAN

'Only a Broken Flask'

Only a broken flask,
But through her love
A fragrance stole upon the evening air,
And Christ was honoured there.

Only a broken loaf,
But from His hands,
A food sufficient for the souls of men
Was offered to them then.

Only a broken life,
But from that Cross
A love to save the world went forth in power,
Born of His darkest hour.

A flask, a loaf, a life with love infused –
Are all things broken that are greatly used?

PETER ISACKÉ

Spring Uninvited

Spring entered January recently
and mosquitoes appeared and danced
their first and last dance on air.
A butterfly, bewildered, sunned itself on ice;
now its wings are frozen.
Catkins killed brown colour
dangling their water droplets in the rain.
Green knives stabbed the earth's surface but stopped,
for a crinkling white savage appeared
and proclaimed his dominance over the earth;
Jack was back and the Spring left quietly.

PETER ISACKÉ

Travelling Voice

What shall I do with the sun and the moon
give them a voice that they might sing?
give them my voice that can make the choice
where it may travel to?
Perhaps it will land in the life burning mass
and shimmer like glass
or pass over grass with the sunbeams.
Maybe it will twitter in the holes of the moon
blinking in time to the silence,
or giving a lullaby to the black crater hole's
soul and the sense of its wholeness.
What shall I do with the sun and the moon
give them a voice that they may sing?

ETHEL JACKSON

'Derry Revisited

It is Sunday morning, Lord,
    And we have been told to go up to Your House with joy.
But this morning, You must understand,
    I come with anger – bitter, brooding anger.
Look, Lord, just look what they have done to our city.
    They've bombed it, Lord:
Have you seen the crumbling rubble?

Stone on dead stone has not even the animation
    To accuse the passer-by.
It all looks like a cardboard scene from a film, Lord,
Where some giant dinosaur has eaten the tops off all the buildings,
    Leaving rubble, ruins and bodiless facades.
Do something, Lord, hit back for me, before I do it for myself.

It is Sunday morning, Lord,
    And I cannot go up to Your House with joy.
I cannot go up to Your House.
To destroy like this someone, somewhere, once felt as I do now:
    Angry, bitter and violent.

Lead me back among the ruins, Lord,
    Lead me back till I find the ghost of my enemy,
    My brother.
Then join my hand to his, Lord,
    And,
    Lord,
    Then,
Forgive us both.

DEREK JONES

Terminal Two

The airline ticket in your hand
Flutters, like my heart.
We both stare awkwardly at the floor,
Our eyes not wanting to meet
In case one or other of us
Should read the agony there.

All around us there is movement.
Other travellers passing by,
desperate to catch their flight in time,
Failing to see the two of us
Sitting quite still, trying to postpone
The evil moment till the last.

We punctuate the silences
With bursts of nervous speech
(Strange how we were always able
to make conversation before)
About how it'll only be for a few months
And then everything will be fine again,
Of course it will – and if ever
I wished I could sleep for a year
It is now.

Your flight is called again,
A very correct voice, female, slightly foreign,
Announcing from somewhere above our heads
That this is the final call
And would passengers please proceed
To gate so-and-so.
And so, the moment we've both
Been waiting for, both been dreading,
Is suddenly over very quickly;
An urgent embrace, and then I watch

As your back slowly recedes down the corridor,
I hope your cases aren't too heavy.
You look around, wave – then turn the corner
And leave me to myself.

Suddenly, we are no longer a couple;
Suddenly we seem to be two individuals,
Just as we were at the beginning;
Already I don't like it,
You are coming back, aren't you?

HILDA M. JONES

White Cherry Blossom Tree in Bud

Chelsea

Sometimes
creative Breath
with pursed lips
puffs promises
even to the finger tips,
fusing the ethereal and the earthy
into such union
even these eyes can see
spirit exists.

KIM W. JONES

Ms N.

Give me no shelter,
Damp warmth of a shack
That impedes the view.
No shade;
I walk bare-headed.
No arm;
Protection's slave I never.

Offer no retreat,
It is anachronism;
I have three parents.
No dovecot;
Child mother I will not.
If dove I find my home among
Among the crags.
No escape;
Eat ashes I cannot
My life's mourning.

Why cry
Not to be petted
But heard.
Do not stoop
But love from rib to rib.

WILLIAM KAY

Welsh Holiday

On a small island lies a graveyard
where the descendants of a small Welsh town
are buried beside tidal waters;
glinting mud bared around

the scene provides nostalgic beauty.
Seabirds dart for food while travellers
walk among the stone slabs
idly. The dates and names signify

patriotism, tragedy and shy love.
A woman nearly forty marries
her curate and dies in childbirth.
Another inscription mutely carries

a family tale of staggered grief.
One son lost in the First War,
another in the Second. Yet more faintly
than the mason's chisel and saw

a pair of lovers have scratched a heart
on one of the slate stones
because, thinking only of each other, they
forgot the island, the mud and the bones.

CLIVE LANGMEAD

Night Watch

Alone,
Before You and the world.

The small hours watch leaves me standing,
A solitary speck on a speckless sea,
A single mind alert for possibilities
That none, save You, can see.
A chance to lean and think and contemplate the sky,
and daunt the mind with those age-old fears
Of Your immense display.

Some peace here Lord, I know.
Some quiet . . .
Even so, I'm not at rest,
I must concern myself with cares:
Of home, of life, of ladders of success . . .

Lord,
I know I need them not,
And yet . . .

Help me to take the silence of this night
Into my soul,
and trust, in peace, until the coming of the Light.

GEORGE LESLIE LISTER

A Cry at Christmas

Christmas comes round again: a magic time
for children, and for those who, still
youthful at heart, see it through children's eyes.
A time of fun and feasting, with a child –
The Holy Child – the centre of it all.

King in a manger,
Godhead made flesh.
A child.

With heads bowed in awe,
Let us kneel to this child
Whose dying will redeem mankind
Through love.

Maybe the days of tinsel and carols,
dancing, and kisses under the mistletoe,
will shut out pictures that come unbidden
of children starving, or charred by napalm bombs
in the name of the civilisation we profess.

Child in a Belfast street,
Caught in the crossfire.
A child.

With heads bowed in shame,
Let us kneel to this child
Whose dying will condemn mankind
Through hate.

CYRIL LLOYD

Spring Sonnet

The lilac bush puts forth its purple spikes
and pink-tipped blossom decks the apple tree,
while on the ground the bright-faced primrose likes
to highlight shaded violet's modesty;
and on the cherry bough full-throated thrush
sings out in answer to the cuckoo's call,
and over all the earth the first fair flush
of Spring unfolds its beauty to enthral.
In full accord but by more wondrous means
the Holy Spirit quickens all that lives
and like Spring's sun on many-shaded greens
new Life to people's varied natures gives.
And as Spring blooms are rendered safe from frost
may God save us from sin, else we are lost.

CHARLES LOVELL

Good Friday Thoughts

Three hours we sat; heard Christ's few words
        Expressed at human length.
Once more with them the dying son
        Gave all his strength.

Beyond me, in their prime, were two
        Who seemed a childless pair.
No movement of their frames relieved
        Their frontward stare.

Her firmer, willed rigidity,
        As if encased in air,
Showed like a hid resentment born
        Of bitter care.

Together separately they sat,
        Drawn by Christ's loneliness,
But each alone betraying all
        His selflessness.

RUPERT LOYDELL

'Sun Beckons'

Sun beckons,
travel for me
as I burn for you.

Wind calls,
follow me
as I sweep the way.

Rain seduces,
drink deep
as I flood your mind.

Moon whispers,
dream for me
as I melt the night.

Time commands,
press on regardless
as I erode you.

Death is silent,
stands waiting,
leaning in the doorway,
green shadow from the exit sign.

DORIS MANNING

Patterns

Beautiful and finely woven
was the rug she showed to me,
created by herself with skilfulness and art;
bright and dark colours
each with the other joining
to make a neat pattern
and a perfect whole.

And thus I was reminded
of life's pattern:
its background formed by our initial years,
strong threads of love and friendship
interweaving with gay and sombre colours of experience,
each pattern quite unique;
and ours, as yet, unfinished.

DORIS MANNING

Every Eye Sees

Who would call a cabbage lovely?
Maybe a market gardener,
surveying his ordered rows with satisfaction;
the barrowboy anxious to sell his wares
to bargain-hunting housewives;
or a cook making a sharp incision
into a prime specimen
to reveal the cream-coloured heart.

Today I have seen a thing of great beauty,
a flower fit to grace the palace of a queen;
deep mauve at the centre
its petals shaded to a picot edge of lavender.
An azalea I thought,
perhaps a begonia, or an exotic hibiscus;
no! an ornamental cabbage.

How wise the ways of the Creator,
to make of one family two such varieties,
and we must learn
neither to scorn the one as mundane
nor to worship the other as beautiful,
but appreciate them both
for their intrinsic value.

DORIS MANNING

Rain

Constant and unremitting as a nagging tone
rain falls in ceaseless torrents from the skies,
streams swell to rivers, rivers turn to flood,
and Man is helpless till the torment dies.

As sharp and cutting as some young wife's tongue
swiftly comes rain, stinging the face and hand,
then, just as sudden as her rage is done,
see how the sun shines golden on the land.

As sweet and tender as a young girl's tears
gently drops rain upon the earth's soft bed,
as when her tears are dried the maid is gay
so blooms the land with flowers the rain has fed.

RANDLE MANWARING

Pine Forest

(In memoriam – K.A.M.W.)

Among the towering pines
of perennial pride,
falling but not fallen,
the mossy path astride,
adding a new dimension,
one leans across the ride.

Caught at sixty degrees,
it makes a special mark
with shafts of angled light
in the criss-cross dark,
dead among the living,
lying bark to bark.

When will it fall completely,
all support withdrawn
by neighbour pines,
their roots outworn,
on a brushwood couch
to be stripped and sawn?

We stand together now,
silent among the trees,
wondering at the limit
of life's harmonies,
as the wind, passing over,
another death decrees.

RANDLE MANWARING

Standing Committees

They seldom stand for long
Or for much,
Leastways for propositions
On which they sit
Indefinitely.

They often shoot the bull,
Then pass the buck,
Sign three copies and sit
On their tails. They take minutes
And waste years.

MURIEL McNAIR

Ipsissima Verba?

You are the salt of the earth.
Gather it together in heaps
lest it be polluted;
keep it in the jar.
Let society rot in its sin
and be redolent of its putrefaction –
the saints in their pristine whiteness
shall be gathered together
as a memorial pillar to me.

You are the light of the world.
Guard it carefully
lest the dark puts it out.
Build a beautiful shrine
for the lamp of God
where it may be kept safe
for you to admire.
Do not take it into the storm
to look for the lost:
the wind might blow it out.
Let the lost look out for themselves –
if they are lucky they will see
the chinks of light through the shutters
and try to come in.

You shall be my witnesses,
so witness faithfully
on Sundays, come what may,
and at as many meetings as you can
give money, make long prayers, sing hymns,
and listen to sound sermons.
Teach my lambs, in particular,
to get their priorities right
and keep the fold nice and tidy:

then it will be easy to find you
when I come back, already gathered
from the rest
and glorifying God in your holiness.

You are my body.
Treat it gently, keep it warm,
make sure it gets enough to eat
and lives respectably.
Keep it out of politics of course
and the crush of common people.
Avoid confrontation
with the realities of evil.
One crucifixion was enough.

VERONICA MEDD

Wind of Heaven

Branches of trees twisting, bending;
Glass panes rattling, shaking;
Outside, buffeted, beaten,
I am unable to stand against you
Great mighty wind.

I am disturbed, frightened even,
But helpless against your strength.
You drive me on, struggling, spent.
Sleepless or breathless, you hold me
Dread, powerful wind.

Yet sometimes you are a gentle breeze.
Your freshness revives me,
Carries me tenderly, lightly, a leaf
Lifted high above the ground
By you soft wind.

Penetrating breath of heaven
Blow me where you will, that
Bending without breaking,
I may go, unresisting, on the road
Meant for me, O Wind.

DAVID MIDDLETON

'It Was As If'

It was as if
The sun were at last returning
To this earth, in slow majesty
Down through the vast space rolling
His ponderous path of flame –
So glows through the morning mists
Beaded with dew, heavy among the trees
The gentle warmth of dawn light,
As if another day could dawn
In this place.
Garden of sepulchres, at the end of the winter
Empty and barren, all that summer brought
Withered and vanished. Emptiness.

Mary, you came through the gate where night lingers
Into this sudden stillness, came very slowly
A fluctuating silhouette, trailing through
Tides of mist and the cold dew,
Gripping your frozen spices –
Is it not strange of all this emptiness,
The depth of hopelessness,
That the last emptiness,
Should mean the height of hope?
One bare place in all this barrenness
Should bring to birth new life
Beyond expectation?

Let not one cold tear startle your cheek,
Look where the body should have been
And see a promise of Paradise.
Gardener? (Indeed, He sowed
Gethsemane with tears)
Now, see at the touch of this Sun returned
To earth, the garden riot with verdure,
Rich with flowers, flowers.

MONA MILLER

Night Sky

Night sky –
star-sequined shawl of dreams
soft flowing over earth
a lover's coverlet
or veil for sorrow's tears.

Night sky –
moon-hatted canopy
or black umbrella'd shade
a candle for the heart
or shelter for misdeed.

Night sky –
a highway to the mind
that searches soul's vast depth
a heavy-lidded eye
that winks and stares at me.

MONA MILLER

Complete

With God's love
 you are a bird singing
  a tree growing
   the wind whistling
    a stream running
     a star shining
      the moon laughing.
Complete.

KEVIN MILLS

Transfiguration

Days all sun-steeped and glorious,
hot with bright flowers
and sweet with fellowship's fruit,
mingle with
days all dark-drenched and aching,
cold without mornings,
and sour with grapes of solitude
in memory's tide.

The soursweet river
sprays into the air
soft light in particles
in an aura of pale yellow time,
suspended around my past,
bringing about a
transfiguration
of my days.

The charcoal spars
of the burnt bridge of summer
crumble on to the paper-white foam
in powder-black sketches
of people and places –
a season depicted with nothing but shadows,
cast in the warm glance
of memory's sun.

FRANCIS AUSTIN MONK

For They Sow the Wind

Hosea 8:7

What are the men of this world?
In seedling hour
what do they see of this world?
The sweet-spun flower.
What will they find in this world?
The sweet is sour

for they sow the wind.

How many men of this world
think they can see
the forest glades of this world
where life may be?
Yet in the wood of this world
they miss the Tree

for they sow the wind
          and shall reap the whirlwind.

FRANCIS NICHOLSON

Of Power and Might

I stretched my hand up to a distant star
And found, like grains of sand, a countless host
That circled into outer space, so far,
My mind in that infinity was lost.
What Power has touched each spinning star with light,
And held the surging waters of the sea,
And caused the earth to rest upon the night,
And blossom form on every fruiting tree?
Within man's face is mirrored God, the dove
Of peace has rested on his head; so shout,
Creation, at this miracle of love.
Our tears will turn to diamonds hung about
The stars and, freely choosing, we shall be
Transfigured in our immortality.

BRENDA NORTON

'On the Death of a Boy'

(written on the death of a boy walking on a lonely road at night, recalling trees he helped to plant in Gloucestershire)

Stripling body
that will never grow again
smashed distorted sudden
without pain
silent breathless still.
   Slain.

Felled in a flash.
Lights flashing.
   Sorrow fell.

Sapling body
bowed swift,
truncated seedless
limbs lifeless lying,
leaves still
a memory
bursting full
potentially mature
with promise,
leaves other saplings
growing on
potentially mature
with seed for sowing . . .

What promise they?
When shall their felling be?
How shall it fall?
Sudden swift unready?
Shall they be
upright tall
full grown towards the Infinite,

seed sown (pure strain)
with fruit a hundredfold?
Or stunted twisted weeping
following the wind
and at the felling
left behind
all promise spent
and fruitless seed?

JANICE NUTLEY

'Real Love'

Real love
long love
pure love
strong love
God's love
true love
deep love
full love
Great love
this love
my love
His Love

MARGARET ORFORD

Olive Trees

God must have had fun creating olive trees.
To have thought of and made a tree of any kind needed
the supreme Creator,
but then to have decided to make one
so individual
so unique
and to have placed it exquisitely
against the Mediterranean blue!

I see them leading the way down the steep incline to the
rocky shore,
defying description;
trunks twisted and gnarled beyond mere Man's
imagining;
shapes to haunt dreams,
producing their wealth of grey-green silvery leaves
and fruits unlike all others.

I think that God is still amused about the olive trees,
and that his laughter plays amongst their leaves
setting them dancing.

MARGARET ORFORD

The Butterfly

My hands are warm to the butterfly
I am trying to set free.
Delicate, frail creature of beauty,
what can it know of me?
I am outside its comprehension.
It knows sunshine and showers,
darkness and the feel of flowers.
We do not ask it to do the impossible
and know Man.

So we, with God,
who looks with tenderness upon our frailty,
trying to guide us.
Trust him!
He knows the way, and, if we let him,
will open windows,
and, cradling us gently in hands we cannot comprehend,
will lift us up and set us free.

EVANGELINE PATERSON

'And That Will Be Heaven'

and that will be heaven

and that will be heaven
at last   the first unclouded
seeing

          to stand like the sunflower
turned full face to the sun   drenched
with light   in the still centre
held   while the circling planets
hum with an utter joy

                    seeing and knowing
at last   in every particle
seen and known   and not turning
away

     never turning away
again

EVANGELINE PATERSON

For a Friend Dying

When light broadens behind the curtains, and I wake
to my peaceful morning,
my thoughts go at once to you, setting out on your slow
day's business of dying.

In the midst of my life I am living your death, seeing
with your eyes the shining
of sun on the leaf. All day I am keeping pace
with your slow journey

and wishing that those you love may be there to send you
– from love into Love going –
and may you launch out gently into the dark
like keel into water moving.

EVANGELINE PATERSON

Deathbed

Now, when the frail and finespun
Web of mortality
Gapes, and lets slip
What we have loved so long
Out of our lighted present
Into the trackless dark

We turn, blinded,
Not to the Christ in Glory,
Stars about His feet

But to the Son of Man,
Back from the tomb,
Who built fire, ate fish,
Spoke with friends, and walked
a dusty road at evening.

Here, in this room, in
This stark and timeless moment,
We hear those footsteps

And
With suddenly lifted hearts
Acknowledge
The irrelevance of death.

BRIAN LOUIS PEARCE

Credo

I believe in the rushing wind, the tremendous driving
force,
the sudden shaft, the sudden shifting of light, the
interposition
of the Holy Spirit in these human affairs, the
interpolation
of the tributaries, ponds and sources
the watery interfaces
water-sheds and water-forces
the sudden ripple of light
throwing diamonds across the water, turning
us to another quarter;
taking us round with the ebullient stream in another
meander
into the presence of Godhead in these vessels of brittle
clay:
the presence lighting these figures, otherwise fast
disappearing
into a darkness deeper than any of their own making:
turning ahead of them, like the hidden water, and calling.

I believe in the wholly Other, the presence behind the
mere clay of Creation:
the holy and solitary Father, who created us,
by whom we are all met
in the terror and joy of this and every day,
in the middle of every instant
at the centre of every insight
at the first and the last light of this and every I.

I believe in the grace which is daily searching and
reaching us,
which has to be felt to be seen, accepted to be believed,

and which, denied or acknowledged, has always inhabited
us
from the first wrinkle across the ocean, as it ever shall be
in the day and the night-time, out beyond night, beyond
day:
in the beginning, so, now, without end,
the sudden shaft, the ripple of light, like a person beside
me,
nearer than hidden water
turning to speak to me:
the sudden shift, the sound of the water
turning

FERGUS PEARSON

My Electric Fire

I'm sitting in my drawing room
shivering, beside my own pianoforte.
I put on an electric fire, and I am
a little bit warmer. I switch the switch
Down. But the other bar goes out. Out? It must
Be the first bar that doesn't work, and so
With the switch on for the second, the first one
works. Isn't it rewarding and
exhilarating
to have a brain?

CLAIRE PEGG

I Am

I is indelible, inexhaustable, indeclinable,
I is indeed, individual, and utterly indefinable,
I is indefeasible, infinite, indominable,
I is indisputable, the inception, and indeterminable,
I is ineffable, independent, and indescribable,
I is indivisible, indispensable, and indestructable,
I is incessant, and I is no sham,
I embraces all, and the Lord said 'I am.'

CLAIRE PEGG

The Loner

I am the loner,
The one who lives within my mind,
The soul that finds comfort hiding in ripples of thought,
The heart that aches, but knows that solace is exiled
        among imagination,
The spirit wandering free in a husk denied that freedom,
The deep eye of knowledge imprisoned by a dumb
        tongue,
I am always the chrysalis never the butterfly,
For I am the loner.

MARGARET PHILLIPS

The Day I Die

The day I die will be a glorious day!
April I think – or maybe the first of May.
And birds will cry aloud for joy
and life newborn,
that glorious morn –
    the day I die.

And I will walk where fairer flowers
than any earth has seen
grow sweet and wild.
And undefiled the panorama
of my Father's home
will stretch before my wondering eyes.
And with what glad surprise
I shall behold
far fairer than all else
    my Jesus' face.

And all that wondrous place
will centre on his beauty –
    and his grace.

And *this* will be my own –
my very own!
For I'll be home –
    the day I die.

GEORGE PLUCKWELL

How Much I Love You

Love poem to Jean

How much I love you,
Like the very light;
Heralding another dawn,
How true I love you,
Like the night,
Where shooting stars are born.
How much I love you
Let me write the ways;
Like the first warm day of Spring,
When Winter's lease seems far away;
And yellow daffodils ring and sing;
How true I love you,
Like my childhood prayers,
Sweet Christmas and the holly bough,
How well I love you,
Like when Winter caresses Spring,
And she renews her marriage vow.

How much I love you,
Like fine Autumn trees;
Brown leaves upon the cottage path,
My little lime tree by the garden wall,
Stripped of her summer beauty,
Yet enduring well to last.
How well I love you,
Like the lost dreams of youth;
Gone neath the cloud of passing years,
How well I love you,
With that little truth,
The whole world ever hears;
How well I love you,
Like the magic of childish games;
Young swift feet across the meadow,

Happy faces in an April rain,
When joy and laughter seemed forever.
How well I love you,
With all my mortal heart,
Worldly ways and vulnerable flesh;
Like a Soul adrift,
Loving beyond death.

VERONICA POPESCU

Time Was

when we played in its sands as children
watching our naive castles contract
into the narrow chasm
adulthood
never dreaming that
the second half of this hour glass
was an avalanche of fine dust that would
sift surreptitiously through our fingers
clouding the issue, burying us in our own
time.

VERONICA POPESCU

Transcendence

Not for three months, let alone nine
Could Mary conceal His presence –
Nor was Joseph kept in the dark
Before His eruption like the morning star
At midnight breaking in winter –
He dazzled both shepherds and wisemen:
We twelve were all blinded – three years –
Till flesh failed to veil Him, even from us,
In a calm stilled sea, and on one mountain top.
How then could we conspire to cover Him
With heavy human robes – bury Him
In puny feudal powers? Him,
Whose setting the sun mourned,
Whose light Death could not extinguish?
He burst out of that grave, propelled
By resurrection – casting us all before Him
By the blaze of His uprising.

DORIS PULSFORD

For a Holy Place

Blood is upon this ground:

First the blood of the martyr, freely given;
This is the blood of joy;

Then the blood of the worker, straining at stone,
(Lacerations of skin, muscle and bone)
Which is the blood of necessity;

Lastly, there is the blood of sorrow:
Blood of the hungry beating the door,
Of the fallen who were not raised,
Of the wounded who were not healed.

Within the brimming Cup
            The blood
        Mingles with His,
    At every Celebration.

So the stones are quiet and clean
And the stranger finds peace.
Ah peace, which is sharper than any sword!

DORIS PULSFORD

Solbad Hall
Communion

To do the familiar thing
In an unfamiliar place,
To take the Holy Bread
In a hotel room,
    Recalls
    An earlier grace,
    Which from the given silence
    Shapes the Word.

JEREMY PURCELL

Sing Halleluia

(in the Dyke Road Park)

As the sun flickers, through the cherry blossom,
gracefully sprinkling the lush grass
with a warm but gentle light,
the park shimmers.
The colours,
The fragrant breeze,
The happy 'buzz' and chanting of animals
please the senses.
One knows that peace, life and beauty are here
and that this is good: This is God.

MICHEL QUOIST

We Have too Much to Do

Lord, here we are,
out of breath,
out of courage,
and almost out of hope.
Caught between the infinity of our desires
and the limitations of our means,
we're tossed about,
torn,
pulled here and pulled there,
confused,
and exhausted.
So, Lord, here we are,
finally still,
and finally ready to listen.

You've seen how our dissatisfaction has made us suffer.
You've seen how fear has led us astray in choosing our commitments.
You've seen how we were afraid of doing too little.
And you've seen the cross imposed by our limited means.

Lord, make us strong enough to do what we should do
calmly,
simply,
without wanting to do too much,
without wanting to do it all ourselves.
In other words, Lord, make us humble
in our wish and our will to serve.
Help us above all to find you in our commitments,
For you are the unity of our actions;
You are the single love
in all our loves,
in all our efforts.
You are the well spring,
And all things are drawn to you.
So, we have come before you, Lord,
to rest and gather our strength.

MICHEL QUOIST

All

I heard a priest, one who lived the Gospel, preach the
Gospel.
The humble, the poor, were carried away,
The prominent, the wealthy, were shocked.
And I thought that such preaching of the Gospel would
soon
frighten away many of those now filling the church,
and
attract those now shunning it.
It occurred to me that it is a bad sign for a follower of
Christ
to be well thought of by conventional 'Christians'.
Rather, it would be better if we were singled out as crazy
or
radical.
It would be better if they pursued us, signed petitions
against us,
tried to get rid of us.

This evening, Lord, I am afraid.
I am afraid, for your Gospel is terrible.
It is easy to hear it preached,
It is relatively easy not to be shocked by it,
But it is very difficult to live it.

I am afraid of deluding myself, Lord.
I am afraid of being satisfied with my decent little life,
I am afraid of my good habits, for I take them for
virtues;
I am afraid of my little efforts, for I take them for
progress;
I am afraid of my activities; they make me think I am
giving
myself.

I am afraid of my clever planning; I take it for success.
I am afraid of my influence, I imagine that it will
        transform lives;
I am afraid of what I give; it hides what I withold;
I am afraid, Lord; there are people who are poorer than I;
Not so well-educated,
    housed,
    heated,
    fed,
    cared for,
    loved.
I am afraid, Lord, for I do not do enough for them
I do not do everything for them.

I should give everything,
I should give everything till there is not a single pain,
        a single
    misery, a single sin in the world.
I should then give all, Lord, all the time.
I should give my life.

Lord, it is not true, is it?
It is not true for everyone,
I am exaggerating, I must be sensible!

Son, there is only *one* commandment,
For *everyone*:
You shall love with *all* your heart,
            with *all* your soul,
            with *all* your strength.

MICHEL QUOIST

I Want to be Somebody

Lord tonight I ask you, once and for all, to rid me of my concern about the impression I make on other people.

Forgive me
For being so preoccupied
with what I seem to be,
with the effect I produce,
with what others think and say of me.

Forgive me
For wanting to imitate others to the extent that I forget
who I am,
For envying their talents so much that I neglect to
develop my own.

Forgive me
For the time I spend playing games with my 'personality'
and for the time I don't spend in developing my character.

Now, let me forget about the stranger that I was
so that I may find my self;
for I will never know my home unless I leave it,
and I will never find myself if I refuse to lose myself.

Lord, let me be open to my brothers,
so that, through them, you will be able to visit me as
your friend.
For then I will be the person that your Love wants me to be,
your son, Father,
and a brother to my brothers.

ANTHONY ROSE

Trouble Is

Trouble is,
I've quite forgotten
when lives were burned and loved-ones cried at home.
Forgotten that daisies and poppies, brushed by the wind,
grow on earth fought for with blood and pain,
and nothing but pride was gained.

Trouble is,
I can see it all on the screen before my glazed eyes,
and eat my tea at the same time,
because really I'm quite used to it now,
comfortably conditioned, nicely positioned by the fire,
and the war-film and the news are no different from each
other.

Trouble is,
I've quite forgotten how to cry,
for I'll never die like those others.
It could only happen over there,
so don't scare me with stories of hatred on my doorstep –
I've seen that on my screen as well.
Others made the world a better place,
at another time,
and the bruised eyes
and the gaping wounds of children
only happen on film.

ANTHONY ROSE

Epitaph to Poetry

They thought they were doing well
Until their rhymes began to grate,
Their stanzas to elongate
Into sad monologues of injustice.

They thought they were doing well
Until their metaphors mixed with the garbage of the
earth,
Their similes became unlike anything recognised as pure,
Their epithets grew loud and arrogant,
Their verbs became inward-looking or violent.

When sentence was passed
It was too late to change.
Then they came to a full-stop
And all asked what it was.

'What phrase does it end?' they said,
'Is it in praise of our lines?'
But it only read 'The End',
And the page grew darker
As the book was closed.

ANTHONY ROSE

In This Dark Night

In this dark night
when demons are dancing round the moon
when trees and wind conspire to bring me down
to lower depths than ever before
O will I ever feel the peace
in this dark night?

In this dark night
when others laugh and joke
and I choke on tears of lonely days gone by
on memories of pain
and a future I know nothing of
O will I ever see the light
in this dark night?

The dank air around my thighs
the whisper of cold on my shoulders
and in my hidden depths a deeper chill
and yet a sigh
a cry
to something beyond the blindness
of this dark night.

JANE ROSE

Old Man

Old Man, I saw you today
sitting alone –
muttering dark thoughts;
grey hands fumbling
with tattered coat,
adjusting string, doing up pins,
watching . . . waiting . . .
for what?
for whom?

Jumbled words, mumbled movements
make up your day –
what do you think
as the world avoids you?
Do you care
that no one dares meet your eye
fearing lest he finds
the real you?

All I know, as I watch
you shuffle away, is that
He whom I'm supposed to follow
would not have passed by
without smiling on you
and making you clean.

PETER SCOTT

Brent Tor

This was Satan's land,
This heaped volcanic pile
Now strewn with foxgloves;
This was Devil's strand
When men's green bile
Oozed forth to moonwatch.

Now God has claimed it,
Strained it, stained it,
Not with martyrs' blood but
Scent of worship.

High now stands Michael's mount,
Love's fount, life's count;
A quiet sanctuary from
Moor's strong storms;
Rude forms transform
Material clay to spirit.

PETER SCOTT

The Night Before

Woolsoft pink on evening sky
As still night air sharpens the twilight sounds;
Cirrus, tugging across a darkening treescape, are
High-flying heralds of a brighter dawn.

Pinpoint of starlight, Saturn's beams,
Punctures the skyline, and
Startles brooding reveries to listen;
Then Maker's tones arrow forth to heartland as
Mares' tails shadow away.

That other Light has come,
Broken into souls' settling darkness;
No need now of lesser lights that
Lamp the shadowlands.

JOCELYN SEMPER

Solution

I cannot see your working
But still you go on, planning and purposing for my life
I cannot see the point of the sorrow
But you blend it to bring harmony in my life
I cannot clearly see your answers –
This does not stop you fulfilling them
And though I cannot see the way ahead,
You know it, and you guide me.

The obedience sometimes doesn't seem to bring results
But as its savour rises to you, you repay
And when the trouble never seems to end
Thank you that you see a day
Of rest ahead; and in the battle
Thank you for the courage to go on.

Lord, I know it costs,
It costs me to shoulder my cross daily and follow you
It costs me to give up people, take up people for your
        sake
It costs me in my heart to surrender to all your claims
Yet the taste of life is sweeter when it's done.

I cannot see the morning,
But the path belongs to you –
And my glad songs that were sad songs
Will re-echo with the praise
Of the living Lamb who keeps me
All my days, all my days.

HOWARD SERGEANT

Strategy

Wiser, no doubt, to think of war in terms
of shaded maps, observing with what ease
the black and strictly impersonal line ploughs
deeply, reaping a harvest of towns – the names,

if tongue can sheave them, yours to string upon
the day's unwieldy talk; safer to count
the score in planes without extravagant
recourse to actual cost in minds or men.

Yet, for all your fables, you cannot avert
the untenable moment of knowing. Tidy
on wind and spiralling height, the falcon already
prepares its tearing descent to your heart.

Since every combatant's wound is your wound, too;
for every death, life pins the guilt on you.

M. BERYL SHEDDEN

Brooding

It was a grey day
a sad day,
for so much had gone before.

The hills
heaved sullen shoulders
to the angry sky.
Pale, wan fingers of sunlight
spreading over the plain
caressed the trees;
but comfort there was not
in their impassioned touch;
and the tree-girt knolls
humped black against the silvery ribbon
of the channel;
stubborn, in an unresponsive silence
which was broken only once in a while
by the melancholy wail
of a seagull
lamenting the days that had been.

A weary wind stirred
the tired grasses
to a whispering resistance,
and rustled
through brown and withered bracken.
The heather
spilt her royal mourning
o'er the upper slopes.
Whilst, here and there
a patch of gorse
bravely kept its smile,
despite the damp depression
of the day.

Grey and swirling
was the sky.
White, immovable,
those granite chunks
tossed out upon the hilltops;
cold and unaffected
by the scowl
of raging clouds ever surging
onwards,
upwards,
towards their black valhalla
out beyond that hard line
of the distant
saddleback.

A tiny speck moved down that line,
Two specks, one streaked with white
And, as
nearer and nearer they came,
brown velvet
poured like liquid
down and over the dusky slopes,
flashed past
with a thunder of hooves
and away, across the purple hills
to the valley below.

A dog barked in the village.
A gull called in reply.
The wind hushed its sighing,
and the mist came,
and the rain came,
and night crept over the land.

M. BERYL SHEDDEN

Storm

It is raining in the forest
    Wearily, drearily,
Spit, spit, spitting on the rustling leaves.
Softly kissing bracken
    Warily, charily,
Drip, drip, dripping on the cold, wet trees.

It is raining on the river
    Moodily, broodingly,
Splash, splash, splashing while the willows moan.
Beating up the surface,
    Madly, savagely,
Dash, dash, dashing it to muddy foam.

It is raining on the hilltops
    Mistily, wistfully,
Churn, churn, churning into grey banks of cloud.
Swathing every summit
    Fearfully, tearfully,
Swirl, swirl, swirling in a soft, damp shroud.

But His sun is beaming somewhere,
    Cheerfully, hopefully,
Warm, warm, warming all the cold, wet fields.
Drawing out the fragrance
    Gently, insistently,
Shine, shine, shining over all earth yields.

M. BERYL SHEDDEN

Disappointment

Do you remember
That cool, dark path within the forest's shade,
Damp with the rain of many hours,
Sweet with the scent of many flowers?
And you were sorry
It was not quite the same – that grassy glade;
The velvet sward was all but fled,
And there the thistle reigned instead.

Only the bracken
Raised jewelled fronds to greet the welcome rain.
Why did you turn away so sad?
Could you not see the trees were glad?
Did you not know then
Life plays its tricks again and yet again;
All that we love must suffer change
And what is dear grow sad and strange.

TIMOTHY STOKES

The Magi

'They offered him gifts: gold and frankincense and myrrh.' Matthew 2:11

I, whose twisting veins run red,
  ardent desire converging on the four chambers of dust,
Climb the rugged mountain.
Where grey-black sky and wind-uprooted grasses
  surmount the pitted boulder.
So I must follow, wary of disturbing the drowsing scree
  on these jagged slopes.
Lest each flint becomes a drop, the drops of a stream,
  and the gentle streams a rampant flood; which hurls
  eddying waters over me.
But now the course fuses with a blazing star,
  which urges me on beyond dark horizons.
Day's searing heat tears, exposing naked flesh.
Night's cold tendrils curl, holding me in their grasp.
I, whose black hair fades,
  unveiling a furrowed head above the greying brows,
Age in my wandering.
For I know not the journey's end.

I, who cried out often to the mutable sea,
  soft cadences echoed by the lapping waves frozen
  in a glassy shell,
Talk to the wind.
Prophesy to the wind, mortal man.
It rages on over shifting yellows and
  tossed couch-grass.
They shall be deaf; though their ears hear.
They shall be blind; though their eyes see.
Bleached dry bones rattle in death's umbered valley.

Herod might rend his purple robes in sorrow
  if he knew of the disfigured servant or the
  bloody tree.
Time shall leech Israel's stream,
The foaming waters are Jerusalem's grave.

I, whose tallow-soaked wick burns low,
  north-wind bends the smoky flame,
Cover the flickering light.
Lest stifling darkness engulfs the flowing wine,
  the banquet food and the carved oak table.
Naked, blind at the moment of birth.
Suckle the breast issuing the milk of human kindness.
Naked, blind at the moment of death,
Cast off garments holding worldly toil.
Walk hand in hand with the scythe and seed,
  which withers away as dark soil breaks open.
But from the white roots voices call;
  forked is the tongue of plough and sword,
  forked is the tongue of the writhing snake,
  forked is the tongue of my genesis.

VAUGHAN STONE

Nineveh

Ring the doom of Nineveh,
Utter forth the condemnation,
Publish God's dread proclamation,
Sound the trumpet's warning call;
E'er the fearful fate shall fall
Leaving dust and devastation,
Plunged in terrible damnation;
Ring the doom of Nineveh.

Sing the joy of Nineveh,
Rising from her bed of ashes
Fling the sackcloth from her members,
Penitent for what is past;
Pure, unbridled joy at last
Springing from the solemn embers
Into every corner flashes;
Sing the joy of Nineveh.

VAUGHAN STONE

Must I, Lord?

And must I love my brother, Lord?
He hates my guts and fears my fettered power;
He clutches tight his hard-won gold and watered garden.
And must I love him, Lord?

And how can I show my love, Lord God?
He loathes me though and dreads my presence;
My skin condemns me. Must I leave him
If I would love him, Lord?

And must I leave him sunk in self?
Does love demand I leave him in the grip of gold
And go and starve myself in Bantustan,
And let his conscience sleep?

And must I renounce the kinship, Lord?
If so, then also his (or mine) with Thee –
Or else the whole creation is a hoax
And words are liars.

Or must I insist? And insist?
My cherished kinship, Lord, with Thee
Rasping his sleepy conscience day by day
Until it wake?

PHIL STREETER

The Garbage Bin

Bean tins, egg shells, tea bags, potato peelings,
sodden paper and broken glass
clattered into our garbage bin
which wheezed with surprise
as I stamped my foot on its fly-freckled assortment
in a search for more space.
Thankfully, two days later,
the bin was empty:
the fetid debris having been humped off
to a faraway rubbish dump where
dogs pad,
cats wash silently in the sunshine
and sparrows argue among dust and paper.

Jesus,
I come to you tonight
with all the muddled rubbish of my life
feeling so soiled,
so crushed,
sick with myself.
It's been a gruelling day
and the rubbish which I tip and pile and press
on you
has made me feel twenty years older;
has caused me to hate myself for loving myself
more than you;
has resulted in a longing to be more naive
and unaffected instead of
enlightened, cultured and professional
(as I sometimes consider myself to be);
has made me wistful of slipping far away
from the public glare into obscure nonentity.
I cry out to you tonight Jesus
because of broken resolutions;

temptations I thought I had the power to play with;
loss of patience when you were alive within me;
help me Lord!
Please help me,
because reeking rubbish is scattered everywhere
in the backyard of my heart
and I feel in such an awful muddle.
I am filled to overflowing Lord –
collect me.

PHIL STREETER

You are so Extravagant Jesus

You are so extravagant Jesus –
unbelievably extravagant in everything you do.
You made a superabundance of things that are
considered
of little value.

How many cast a second glance
at sunrises and sunsets?
Yet
both go flaunting around the skies
like women parading new dresses.

How many of us bother our heads
about a field filled with varnished buttercups?
We can't eat them.
Yet
you find buttercups so cheap and fascinating
to produce
that golden carpets flop around everywhere.

Then
there are the huge heaving seas.
Why make so much water Jesus?
We can't drink it.
And
all those snowflakes
endlessly parachuting to earth.
Why send so many
and why each one a different pattern and shape?
Sheer extravagance.

No Jesus
you are by no means economical.
Even a picnic on a hill
resulted in twelve baskets filled with leftovers.

When Mary of Bethany was extravagant in her worship
of you
people cried
'Economise!'
You said,
'This woman's extravagance
will be praised and remembered for ever.'

Yes, my younger brother,
you are beginning to glimpse
a hue in the rainbow of My character:
creation demonstrates
My extravagance
and may be considered outlandish
preposterous
yet it symbolises My love
for you.

Commonsense is finite
a companion of timidity
and timidity produces
economy.

I was not sensible
or calculating
or precise
when I loved you
from that hillside.

Economy takes no risks.
Without venture
there can be no adventure.

I tell you
My younger brother
that, alongside wealth,

economy has been deified.
However,
I make no allowances for
cutting cloth accordingly,
nor for hoarding for rainy days;
you must give yourself extravagantly.
The security
in the apparent wisdom of economy
is opposite to the nature of My Father
who delights in feeding millions of birds
with billions of insects;
Who cultivates grasses
and invents flowers
simply for the joy of it.

KIM TAPLIN

Church Communion

They said I'd find God here!
Cold as if to defy the 'Other Side'
With terrestial kilowatt and dark
Disciplined oak daring comfort.
I join the human dots, contagiously
Spaced, their anonymity preserved by the
Security of quiet inner prayer.
Hymnal verse is choked by a two-stroke
Crescendo, and a child's shrill
Vibrato constricts her mother in a
Strait-jacket of embarassment.
They said I'd find God here.
The procession meanders agoraphobically;
A Harvest gift atones for conscious
Guilt as right hand seeks Narcissian
Solace left.
Eyes are gagged for they give too much
Away, allowed only to humbly inspect the
Carpet during the retreat from the blitz
Gazes to the safe, prayer-postured
Camouflage of the wooden Trench.
As I glance at the silver 'wishing well'
Spotted with copper . . . it dawns on me . . .
That's why they're so stingy on the heat!
They said I'd find God here?

KIM TAPLIN

The Rulin' Class

beerboozinmoneylosin
pornoreadineverbleedin
crudejokeinnose-in-pokin
radiooneinlots-a-funnin
fishandchipsinwatchclocktickin
mickeytakingfriendshipfakinstrikemakin . . .

PROLETARIAN!!

KIM TAPLIN

Variety (is the Spice of Life)

monday, work, eat, TV, sleep, tuesday,
work, eat, TV, sleep, wednesday, work,
eat, TV, sleep, thursday, work, eat,
TV, sleep, friday, work, eat, cinema,
take away, sex, sleep, saturday, over-
time, eat, grandstand, drink, dance,
drink, drink, hic, vomit, deep sleep,
sunday, sleep, headache, alka, rest,
eat, play, snooze, TV, sleep, monday . . .

'Sobriety is the vice of life.'

R. S. THOMAS

Persons

A new member lifts up his heart
to be counted in the birdless streets
of a town, the hairs of his head
complicating the working
of the heavenly computer. A well-used name
is assigned him; when it is called
he only replies.
                        I have walked the gallery
of a million faces and encountered
no doubles, pausing sometimes
as though in recognition
of a likeness to be rebuked
by the soul, the offended spirit
trapped in its frame.
                        There is a palette
that knows no limits to the colours
that can be mixed on it; always
they blend, yet out of them the selves
rise, different, detached, each
with the mark of its identity
upon it. There must be a place
for their keeping, an entelechy
rather that is beyond time
and space and independent
of number: a texture, a
way of looking, a peculiar smile.

PHIL THOMSON

On the Marsh at Kinfauns

This was an occasion
for silence.
First, the thick mist rising
off black water,
the tall grass leaning stark
against dark rocks
and the baffle of first light.

A thin cry of gulls
scraped the stillness,
the bank lurched
and from her stiff mooring
a heron,
with the startling slow motion
of wing upon water,
rose to tangle
with a shifting sky.

PHIL THOMSON

I am Familiar with the Movement of Sparrows

I am familiar
with the movement of sparrows;
they argue between buildings,
sing in graveyard trees.
But I question the authority of starlings:
they darken the walls;
their loud dusk warning
urges the traffic skyward.

Hearing that, in another city
in someone's flimsy cage
you plait your hair,
hide your thin white ankles under silk
and talk of angels,
I am beginning to understand
the flight of fancy.

Use up all the sky you want,
go where you desire –
flying does not make you free
it only takes you higher.

PHIL THOMSON

Bridge

Broken glass and bits of dolls
and messages in chalk
so this is how the other half,
this is how the other half . . .
be careful where you walk

Empty frames and rusting cans
and old half-eaten books
so this is how the other half,
this is how the other half . . .
be careful where you look

Rotting doors and dripping walls
and floors you have to watch
so this is how the other half,
this is how the other half . . .
be careful what you touch

another gin? some paté, dear?
whose turn now to deal?
this is how the other half,
this is how the other half,
this is how the other half . . .
be careful what you feel

be careful what you feel my dear
be careful what you feel

IAN TODD

The Lecture Theatre

Drunken in learning
he holds his place
amongst the learned,
his thoughts dissolve
into the seas of education,
his grant is more
than ransom
for an existence.
Well-soiled texts
that reflect his memory,
no ounce of cerebral waste
is held in desolation,
his senses numb
in the echoes of the lecture theatre.
Where is his childhood
of open play?
'We find your talent –
we channel your future',
they say in their
ignorance of power.
He finds his building blocks
behind the attic door
and knocks down his childhood
with a wave of adult understanding,
and in the rubble
he builds his memories
that hold their hidden secrets from him.
The world will measure his stature –
he cannot find a care
warm enough and old enough
down which to escape, it seems
the sea's waves always grind pebbles
and the ideas of his brain
are already washed up
in the sands of time.

MARGARET TUFTON

Kneel and be Thankful

Dead still in the middle of the hard, grey country lane;
The padding dog at stand, his clicking claws quite still
beside me
At dusk.
An owl in its silent wheel sank sweet to a tree
And the quiet broke sharp in a thousand rings
And a pigeon clattered, tumble-tattered, flew
And the discord fell asleep
And the quiet grew.
The dipping lane streamed out, out and the sky, the sky
Held wide its arms,
Its wild and laughing arms.
And the sky was patched and loved
And stretched about with the gentle grey of a pigeon's
breast,
With the faded blue of a linnet's egg,
And the elm trees walked in twos and threes by the way,
Tall and black with leafy clumps
As starkly stuck with floor mops crazy shaken out to dry;
And over far
The charcoal-coloured cardboard hills
Were stabbed by rows of needle-pricks and lights peeped
through.
The bats played tag beneath the darkening oak,
Dived through the dragging boughs
And squeaked oh! paradise high for glee.
A grasshopper woke;
Or late to bed he chirped his prayers.
Back high in the east
Among the darker clouds
Some rags of gold flew brave;
Then from the church the clock struck ten
And in a deep blue tear,
Madonna blue,

Shone one bright star, so clean, so clear, so piercing
bright so small.
Amid the depth.
A seagull cried alone.
The wind blew up and in the hedge
The ghostly nettles bowed before the music,
Whispered twice
And danced a stately minuet –
And gently kissed.
A delicate moth flew its life along;
Powder-blurred in the shadowed grass
Pale-dreaming yarrows adored with upturned faces;
And bumble-toppled clover heads, milk white, gave
benison;
And praise was all
And leapt and sang
And shouted without voice
Danced
Into the silent source
Without a sound.
But I heard;
For this life in love I ran mad with joy
And laughed in his arms.

A cold wet nose touched my hand;
Up the hay-wisped path we went home.

CHRIS WALTON

Penultimate

The ultimate, never to use –
Simply to defend.
Power to kill, to agonizingly craze
Millions, never to use –
Merely deterrent.
Opportunity to flick the globe
Out of orbit, not to use
But present for peace.

Globe still held by tarnished thread
Like hope
It spins, orbits smoothly but rocks
Like joy,
In seconds of existence
Bright colours have darkened,
Like love.
Our ultimate broods
Like Nimbus.

Ultimates have killed and gone;
In more seconds are
New ultimates possible?
Or now in our time does
The nimbus break
The colours vanish
The thread snap?

Present in fear, never to use –
Only when necessary.
Breeding suspicion, insecurity
And hate, never to use:
Only next time.
Symbolic of power, of wealth
And of pride, not to use
But present for the obliteration.

ALEX WARNER

Four-letter Words

I believe in four-letter words
of the right kind
  Let a string of them pour
from my lips to shock
to turn heads.

Four-letter words
five-letter words
to turn the air a better colour
than blue.
Words like 'love'
        'holy'
    and 'free'

Free to express
an unusual language
usually spoken in select cloistered circles.
Words of power.

I believe in five-letter words
that shock you
because someone told you
they're from a bygone age
and they sound fanatical
or quaint.
Words like 'grace'
        'peace'
        'glory'
        'faith'
and the most powerful word I know:
        'Jesus'.

NIGEL WATSON

Ships that Pass in the Night

(At a party)

They are an archipelago of people,
Springing from the same bedrock of humanity,
Battered by the same unfathomable seas of life,
Sharing similar horizons, and yet
Never touching.
But, as no one is self-sufficient, they participate in trade,
Exchanging varieties of manufactured phrases.
There are grand fleets full of refined and empty
platitudes.
And bulging cargoes of ornamental gossip,
Dirty holds packed with crude amusements,
And bragging lies in impressive-looking packing.
They import empty rumours and export them as scandal
And redirect the pleasantries without heeding them at all.
They do not want the merchandise but sense a need for
trade,
For only through these dealings do they feel less alone.

My island stands apart
Struggling to be self-sufficient, while dreading isolation,
But despising more the noisy throng of worthless
conversation.
I flounder, adrift in a churning sea of chatter
Amidst the crashing waves of blue jokes and white lies.
Ships pass in the night with belching smokestacks
Hailing each other with hearty voices and dulled
emotions,
Full speed ahead on liquid fuel, and diluted clichés.
Then across the sea of bobbing heads and floating minds
That are drowning in the alcoholic ocean of acceptability
You look at me and offer no devalued words in trade;
But your smile penetrates my import restrictions
And I know my ship has come in.

JEFFERY WHEATLEY

Epiphany

('. . . angels bending near the earth
To touch their harps of gold.'
Edmund Hamilton Sears 1810–76)

Thank you
Edmund Hamilton Sears
for your carol about the song of angels,
Thank you, Fra Angelico
for the feather detail in their wings.

Were your pipes frozen
Christina Georgina Rossetti
that you wrote of bleak mid-winter,
earth like iron, snow on snow
and water like a stone? Gas-fired
my central heating keeps the ice out.

Who's that knocking?
A king with a gift of aromatic herbs.
The stick insects, for whom parthenogenesis
is a fact of daily life, sway hopefully
on the drying privet in their tank.
We offer wine. His camel chews the roses.

He insists there is a miracle
in this untidy house.

JEFFERY WHEATLEY

The Unicorn

Softly the unicorn
moves through our moonlit wood
head high, eye confident
– no more security
than lies in unbelief –
his capture always difficult
even in legend.

His was the cryptic smile
that rocked St Peter,
shattered Paul
and beggared Islam, kissed
the dark night captain
that the pilgrims followed,
never quite seen.

DICK WILLIAMS

Old Church

The old church takes its place among the streets
Where uncollected pintas stand in sparkling array
Like medals on the bedsocks of the weary folk who stay
In bed, as silent tribute to the other pintas downed
Upon the night before.

Patient and urgent as eternity she stands
Casting an eye along the empty ways
Which separate with silences
The sounds of solemn slumberings
As those who answer to her tolling call
Find, in this quiet morning hour,
These streets to be the corridors of power.

More than at home with modern truth
In ancient wisdom more than up to date
The old church understands
The spaceships which erupt with human splendour,
The poets who discourse with solemn candour,
the armies which debate with lethal thunder,
the surgeons who perform with modern wonder,
the pride which tears two human hearts asunder,
the virtues and the vices none can number.

And when the sleepy folk at length arise
They'll see her fearless cross against the skies.

DICK WILLIAMS

Middle Age

When I was a child, I thought as a child,
And when I saw an elder sitting
Hands clasped, legs crossed, head tilted,
Immobile on a chair,
I thought he must be doing nothing.
There before me, at that time, I thought would be
The incarnation of vacuity:
An adult shell, a hoary crust
Enveloping a void.

But now I am become a man I put away such childish
things.
Now I sit
Hands clasped, legs crossed, head tilted,
Immobile in a chair,
Quite still within this empty room
While bloodless sunshine breaks the clouds
And till the next autumnal shower
Projects a pallid spotlight on this hour.

Oh could the child who was the Father to this man
Have seen me now!
What lacerating adjectives would crown
The epithets by which he'd make me known
Unto himself.

So, crown, sit velvet barbed upon my brow,
For I know what has forever been
The content of such stillness.

Now as I sit thus unemployed
The stockpiled libraries of the mind
Unship their heavy burdens
On the shores of meditation,

Divulge their hidden riches, disgorge in great processions
The unrelated treasures of the years.

As pallid sunshine probes this empty room
A bloodless omen of storms past and storms to come,
The mind deploys its plunder with delight:
All gold and crimson,
Blazing blues, encyclopaedic greens and musky
Purples, sucked
From a million memories and sensations
Shift slowly to great pressures from the depths
Move marvellously to that resolution of the soul
Which is some small Amen
To that great Word
By which the worlds were made.

The heart is full, the mind is charged, the spirit climbs,
And in this quintessential life
The body rests.
Amen.

SUSAN WILLIAMS

The Bindweed and the Rose

You are the bindweed,
I am the rose;
Your coarse white trumpets shout
Too loudly in my shell-pink ear;
I cannot hear
Bees' hum,
Or feel the sun
Now that your broad green fingers,
Icy flames,
Cover the sky.
I know your faults too well;
Feeble in the air,
And brittle in the ground,
And yet it is your virtues now
Which smother me;
Your length, tenacity.
You wither in the autumn
And I breathe again;
Perhaps next spring
It will not be the same.
I'll grow more thorns.
And so we live,
Antithesis
Of symbiotic love,
Till – death – us – do – part.

Or lion and lamb
Lie down,
And rose and flame
Are one.

SUSAN WILLIAMS

Liverpool Cathedral

When medieval men rejoiced in stone
heaven was near enough to touch, but now
God is galactic,
and we sing his song
in a towering space
which we ourselves have made to honour him,
and find ourselves diminished.

Art and engineering need the natural
constrained in stone and glass,
and light flows down
through tinted animals, translucent leaves,
to glow on walls that grow like pillared oaks
into great curtains dizzy with verticals
that hang in front of the sun.

The whole is a manmade wonder,
now rejoice, look up
and see if God is here
or if he speaks.
Light streams in many colours in this universe
and the organ stirs
a hurricane of sound.

And on the ground a dot of red,
a moving speck of blood,
a ladybird
meandering over the stone.
The organ drowns her footsteps
but her presence signifies
that God is in his temple, he has come.

ROBERT WINNETT

Canterbury

25th March, 1980

Today, in Canterbury, the Church put on
Her festal garb and colourful array
To celebrate the coming to his throne
Of Robert, called by God in this our day
To lead and serve with apostolic care
Those Christians, far dispersed in many lands,
Who find their focus in Augustine's Chair
And now for Robert lift up praying hands.

Through crowded choir and nave, while organ pealed,
A humble man with shepherd's staff he trod,
Whose poise and simple dignity revealed
The strength of one who knew the peace of God:
And when he raised his hand and voice to bless
We caught the accents of Christ's tenderness.

ROBERT WINNETT

To an Agnostic

You say you *don't* believe and that I *do*:
Up to a point that judgment may be true,
And yet it fails to sound our complex state,
For doubt is not faith's foe but is its correlate.

In doubt lies faith that truth is ours to find,
Discovered, not created, by the mind.
By very doubt truth's sovereign claim who own
Are seekers after God, though He remain unknown.

In faith lies doubt for faith is trust not sight,
A trust that in life's darkness there is light,
Light that removes not all uncertainty
But gives us strength and hope to live courageously.

'Lord, I believe: help Thou mine unbelief',
A father prayed whose heart was torn by grief,
A prayer which rose from mingled faith and doubt,
A prayer for you, agnostic, and for me, devout.

VERONICA ZUNDEL

Matins

each morning up
he takes an apple
round green red from that polished bowl.
he holds it hard to his eye against the window.
through this apple
he can see framed out such:
a slice of sky, a cloudstretch,
light on the backs of leaves
and the appleskin spun taut about them still.
he waits time for a leaf to flicker
or cloud to slide along.

and every morning it moves
he writes a different poem.

VERONICA ZUNDEL

Who Killed Steve Biko?

Not I said the judge
with my book never blotted

Not I said the jailer
with my keys held so tightly

Not I said the sergeant
with my gun clean and shiny

Not I said the journalist
with my news fit for printing

Not I said the voter
with my faith in the country

Not I said the President
with my wall-map so tidy

It was I said God
Punish me

Biographical Notes

Caroline Ackroyd Born in Cardiff, lives in Sevenoaks, Kent. Housewife, mother of two children.

Simon Alexander Born in Bristol, lives in Glasgow, Scotland. Anaesthetist. A successful artist whose paintings have been exhibited widely. His book *The Conversion of Mordred* was published in 1979.

Cathy Anderson Born in Kettering, lives in Porthcawl, South Wales. Housewife. Enjoys reading, music, and walking by the sea. Has seen her work published in a number of magazines.

Corrine Bailey Born in Stockport, lives in Birmingham. A housewife and mother of four children. A water-colour artist who enjoys gardening, reading, and the English countryside.

Gordon Bailey Born in Stockport, lives in Birmingham. Writer/broadcaster/youth worker. His books include *Plastic World, Patchwork Quill*, and *I Want to tell you how I feel, God*. Enjoys wildlife, collecting old postcards and attempting to play golf.

John Bampton Born in West Drayton, Middlesex, lives in Peterborough, Cambridgeshire. Retired valuer. Enjoys travel, has a particular interest in railways.

Sheila Barclay (deceased) Born in Croydon, died March 1981. Was married to an Anglican clergyman (Ian has given us permission to retain the work which Sheila submitted). Was chairman of Brighton and Hove Arts Council and was associated with the establishment of The Old Market Arts Centre in Hove.

Todd Barnhart Born in Montana, USA, lives in Newquay, Cornwall. Student of literature.

Richard Bauckham Born in London, now living in Handforth, Cheshire. A university lecturer in theology. Has had several theological books published and has seen his poetry published in various magazines.

Rosemary Bazley Born in Llanberis, north Wales, now living in Kidderminster, West Midlands. Housewife and private language teacher. Has written several books including *Shadow Pantomime, Pride of the Evening*, and *All Things to Enjoy*. Has contributed to a wide variety of magazines as well as broadcasting with the BBC.

Patrick Berthoud (deceased) Born in Offenham, Worcestershire, died May 1979 (his wife Ann has given us permission to retain the work he originally submitted). Was an Associate Dean, Faculty of Arts, Open University. Contributed to a variety of publications.

Sir John Betjeman Poet Laureate. Born in London, now lives in Berkshire. Probably Britain's best-loved living poet. His books include *Ghastly Good Taste, Antiquarian Prejudice, Old Lights for New Chancels, First and Last Loves*, and *A Few Late Chrysanthemums*. Sir John has been, for many years, a regular broadcaster and television personality.

Joan A. Bidwell Born in Barnstaple, Devon, now lives in Hawkinge, Kent. Retired. Lists her interests as design (Joan was a display artist prior to retirement), bird-life, local history and astronomy.

Lynette Bishop Born in Cardiff, now living in Purley, Surrey. A housewife, married to a Baptist minister, mother of three children. Has contributed to several magazines. Enjoys drama, reading and patchwork.

Catherine Bonye Born in Epping, lives in Chislehurst, Kent. Clerical assistant in the Inland Revenue. Has been writing poetry for only three years and hopes to become a novelist.

David Boyd Born in Belfast, lives in Holywood, County Down. Artist. Has seen his work published in various publications. Enjoys mountaineering. Married.

Frank Buchanan Born in Selworthy, Somerset, lives in Godalming, Surrey. Clerk in Holy Orders. Canon Emeritus of Birmingham Cathedral, 1971. Has published both poetry and plays and seen his work appear in many magazines and periodicals. Enjoys country walking and nature studies.

Valerie Budd Born in Berlin, now lives in Romford, Essex. Housewife, mother of three children. Enjoys family life, reading, folk music, the countryside and the sea.

Dorothy Bull Born and still lives in Swindon, Wiltshire. Housewife. Has had her work published in various magazines. Member of the Fellowship of Christian Writers.

Raymond Chapman Born in Cardiff, lives in London. Professor of English Studies at the London School of Economics and Priest in Auxiliary Ministry. Awarded third prize in the Michael Johnson Poetry Competition in 1981. His books include *Early Poems, Prince of the Clouds* (poetry) and *The Language of English Literature, Linguistics and Literature, Faith and Revolt* (academic works). Married with two children.

Petya Christie Born in Widnes, Lancashire, lives in Liverpool. Religious Sister of Mercy/teacher. Enjoys making music (guitar, harmonica, mandolin).

Jack Clemo Born and still lives in Goonamarris, Cornwall. A prolific writer whose works include *The Marriage of a Rebel, The Invading Gospel, Confession of a Rebel, Broad Autumn, Cactus on Carmel*, and *The Clay Verge*. Jack's poetry has been published widely.

Jim Donnelly Born in Omagh, County Tyrone, now lives in Cambridge. Publisher and printer's reader. Married with four children. Has contributed to many magazines. Enjoys local history and religious biography.

Michael J. Douglas Born in Skryne, now lives in Navan, County Meath. Retired clergyman. His book of poems, *Emmanuel*, was published in New York, and he has seen his poetry in various magazines. Enjoys reading and sport.

John Dutton Born and still living in Dudley, West Midlands. Student of music. This is the first publication of John's poetry. Enjoys reading and listening to music.

Sue Elkins Born in London, now lives in Beeston, Nottinghamshire. Student of theology. Has seen her work in various magazines. Enjoys needlework, drawing cartoons, walking and badminton.

Barry Etheridge Born and still lives in Basingstoke, Hampshire. Studying for B.Ed. Was awarded second prize at the 1978 Basingstoke Music Festival for his prose work *Loneliness*. Enjoys soccer (is a qualified FA referee), ornithology and wildlife in general.

Peter Fenwick Born in Eastbourne, Sussex, now lives in Guildford, Surrey. Studying for ordination. Father of two children, his wife died in 1968. Enjoys English and German literature, walking, sailing and swimming.

Peter Firth Born in Stockport, Cheshire, now lives in Bristol. Clergyman and BBC producer. Married with five children. Has received the Seville (Spain) International Radio Open Award for a programme on 'Joy', 1975. As well as contributing to a variety of publications, Peter's first book, *Lord of the Seasons*, was published in 1978. Enjoys photography, writing, people, and has 'a lifelong affair with Manchester United'.

Thomas Foy Born in County Mayo, Eire, now lives in Sligo. Priest. Has contributed to a variety of magazines. Enjoys reading, writing, nature study and local history.

Keith Freeman Born in Nunthorpe, Yorkshire, now lives in Shoreham-by-Sea, Sussex. Insurance claims assessor. Won first prize in the 1977 Brighton Competitive Music Festival. In 1980 his first book of poetry was published: *An Element of Time*. Married, father of two children. Enjoys sport and supports Brighton and Hove Albion.

John Gibbs Born in Harare, Zimbabwe, now lives in Woonton, Herefordshire. Gardener. Married.

Clare Girling Born in Swinton, Lancashire, now lives in Beaumaris, Anglesey. Retired teacher. Married with two daughters. Is interested in wild flowers and trees, enjoys painting.

Mary Goodey Born in London, lives in Camborne, Cornwall. Retired secretary. Has had poetry published. Enjoys nature study, games and reading the Bible.

Lucy M. Green Born in Malvern, Worcestershire, now lives in Lancaster. Retired teacher. Awarded first prizes for poetry by the *Westmorland Gazette* and in the 1975 World Wildlife Poetry Competition. Enjoys gardening, alpine flowers, mountains and birds.

Angela Griffiths Born in Leighton Buzzard, Bedfordshire, now lives in Frome, Somerset. Children's writer. Married, mother of three children. Member of the Fellowship of Christian Writers, and of the Society of Women Writers and Journalists. Enjoys reading and writing.

Sally F. Harvey Born in Wigan, Lancashire, lives in Tewkesbury, Gloucestershire. Housewife and mother. Has had poetry published. Edits a church magazine and enjoys photography, gardening and playing the guitar.

Stewart Henderson Born in Liverpool, now lives in Thames Ditton, Surrey. Writer/poet. Married. Has had two books published: *Carved into a Scan* and *Whose Idea of Fun is a Nightmare*? Has contributed widely to magazines. Has had his poetry broadcast by the BBC and many local radio stations. Often performs his poetry.

Lynda Hingley Born in Coventry, lives in Tupsley, Hereford. Teacher.

Percy Hodges Born in Rodbourne Cheney, Wiltshire, lives in Poole, Dorset. Clergyman. Has had several books published including *The Nature of the Lion*, and *Riches of the Prayer Book* and has contributed to a variety of church publications. Canon Emeritus of Southwark Cathedral.

Michael Hodgetts Born in Birmingham, lives in Sutton Coldfield, West Midlands. Teacher. Has seen his work published in a variety of publications.

Trevor Hoggard Born in Misterton, Nottinghamshire, lives in Cambridge. Training for the ministry. Is interested in soccer, cricket and Morris Minors.

Nesta M. Howard Born in Shortlands, Kent, lives in Bridport, Dorset. Retired teacher. Collaborated in *Penguin Guide to Dorset and Wiltshire* with S. G. Underwood.

Sue Hudspith Born and still lives in Luton, Bedfordshire. Training as a deaconess. Housewife and mother of two children.

Lorna Inman Born in and lives near Bristol. Housewife and mother of three children. Widow. Has contributed poetry to magazines. Enjoys poetry, music, gardening and the countryside.

Peter Isacké Born and lives in Birmingham. A member of The Birmingham Arts Group. Enjoys cycling, country pursuits, theatre, classical music, art and photography.

Ethel Jackson Born in London, now lives in Belfast. Teacher. Has had her work published in magazines. Enjoys reading, playing the guitar, and is a supporter of Arsenal Football Club and Middlesex Cricket Club.

Derek Jones Born in Nuneaton, Warwickshire, lives in Milan, Italy, where he works as a computer consultant. Is learning Hebrew. Plays the guitar.

Hilda M. Jones Born in Seven Kings, Essex, lives in Chelsea, London. Secretary. Life member of the Newspaper Institute of America. Has contributed to a variety of magazines and anthologies. Enjoys, amongst other things, reading, music and photography.

Kim Jones Born in Salford, Lancashire, lives in Highbury, London. Student who is working towards a Ph.D. in the History of Art.

William Kay Born in Margate, Kent, lives in Basingstoke, Hampshire. Educational researcher, University of Southampton. Has seen his writings published in a variety of publications.

Clive Langmead Born in Nairobi, Kenya, lives in Wrotham, Kent. Navigating Officer. First Officer of *MV Doulos* (Christian missionary ship). Married with two sons, his family travels with him. Enjoys flying and audio visuals.

George Leslie Lister Born in Redcar, Yorkshire, lives in Wolsingham, County Durham. Retired Further Education Adviser. His poetry has appeared in a number of magazines. Has a keen interest in local history and archaeology.

Cyril Lloyd Born in Pontypool, Gwent, now lives in Maidstone, Kent. Minister of Religion. Father of three children. Member of Kent County Council's Religious Education Committee.

Charles Lovell Born in London, lives in Rickmansworth, Hertfordshire. Retired civil servant.

Rupert Loydell Born and lives in London. Student. Awarded first prize in the 1978 Richmond Poetry Competition. Edits *Stride* magazine. Enjoys reading, motorcycles, sailing, music, politics and growing cacti.

Doris Manning Born in London, lives in Tunbridge Wells, Kent. Disabled. Has contributed to a variety of magazines. Paints and plays music by mouth.

Randle Manwaring Born in London, lives in Wilmington, Sussex. Author/poet/company director. Has had a number of books published including *The Swifts of Maggiore, Thank You Lord Jesus, In a Time of Unbelief, From the Four Winds*, and *The Heart of this People*. Deputy chairman of Church Society and The Crusaders' Union. Contributes to numerous publications.

Muriel McNair Born and lives in Glasgow, Scotland. Married, mother of three children. Deputy Secretary of the Baptist Union of Scotland. Awarded Edinburgh University Sloan Prize for Scots Poetry, 1954. Enjoys playing and listening to music.

Veronica Medd Born in Newcastle, lives in Penrith, Cumbria. Adviser in Religious Education. Awarded prizes by *Symphony* for poetry in 1978 and 1980/81. Has contributed to a variety of publications. Interests: literature, music and drama; hobbies: walking, swimming and keeping fit.

David Middleton Born and lives in Norwich. Minister of Religion. One book published: *A Time to Unite*. Has contributed to a variety of magazines and has broadcast his verse on radio and television. Enjoys music, painting, sailing and mountain-walking.

Mona Miller Born and lives in London. Secretary. Teacher of dancing. Poetry published and broadcast. Has also published three children's books.

Kevin Mills Born in Bedwas, Rhymney Valley, lives in Blackwood, Gwent. Part-time warehouse assistant. Interests include literature and contemporary music.

Francis Austin Monk Born in Callington and lives in Hayle, Cornwall. Schoolmaster. Won first prize for English Verse, Jack Evans Cup. Interests include: writing, amateur theatre and tapestry.

Francis Nicholson Born in Birkenhead, Merseyside, lives in Cowes, Isle of Wight. Retired. Won the Poetry Cup 1980 and has had his work published in a number of magazines.

Brenda Norton Born in Cardiff, lives in Durham. Teacher/housewife. Enjoys music, natural history, hill-walking.

Janice Nutley Born in Dartford, Kent, lives in Lewes, Sussex. Housewife. Interests include Ancient Egyptian and British archaeology.

Margaret Orford Born in Harare, Zimbabwe, lives in Reading, Berkshire. Writer. Books include *The Royal Mistress, That Beloved Esquire*, and *The King's Daughter* (historical novels). Her poetry has been included in a variety of publications and has been broadcast. Home, family and research for her novels occupy her time fully.

Evangeline Paterson Born in Limavady, Ulster, lives in Leicester. Housewife/poet. Awarded prizes for poetry at the Christian Poetry Festival, London, the 1980 Cheltenham Poetry Festival, and the 1982 Royal Sheffield Institution for the Blind International Poetry Competition. Her books include *Whitelight* and *Bringing the Water Hyacinth to Africa.* A large number of magazines have published her poetry. For five years she ran a monthly poetry workshop at the Arts Centre Group, London.

Brian Louis Pearce Was born and lives in Middlesex. College librarian. His books include *The Argonauts and Other Poems, Selected Poems*, and *The Vision of Piers Librarian.* Has contributed to a wide variety of publications and has wide experience in editing poetry journals. Enjoys chess and local history.

Fergus Pearson Born in Ballymoney, Ulster, lives in London. Multi-media artist.

Claire Pegg Born and lives in Nottingham. Social work student. Some poetry published. Enjoys reading, travel, theatre and cycling.

Margaret Phillips Born in London, lives in Redruth, Cornwall. District nurse. Some poetry published. Lists her interests as 'work, family and church-family life'.

George Pluckwell Born in Enfield, Middlesex, lives in Rowhedge, Essex. His book *Children of the War* published in 1966. His poetry has been published and broadcast widely.

Veronica Popescu Born in Ontario, Canada, now lives in Birmingham. Housewife and mother of three children. Member of The Birmingham Arts Group.

Doris Pulsford Born in London, lives in St Albans, Hertfordshire. Retired teacher. Has won poetry prizes in *The New Statesman.* Her book, *Inner Persuasions*, published 1977. Has contributed to various publications. Deeply committed to voluntary work.

Jeremy Purcell Lives in Brighton. Jeweller.

Michel Quoist Born in Le Havre, France. Priest. Doctorate in Social and Political Science. Was awarded the Prix Jansen of the Societé de Géographie à Paris for his sociological study, *The City and the Man.* Books include *Living Words, Christ is Alive, Meet Christ and Live, Prayers of Life.* Travels widely in Europe leading retreats and conferences.

Anthony Rose Born and lives in Birmingham. Local government officer. Enjoys singing and song-writing.

Jane Rose Born and lives in Birmingham. Insurance underwriter. Married to Anthony. Members of The Birmingham Arts Group.

Peter Scott Born in Southampton, lives in London. Education Secretary of Bible Churchmen's Missionary Society. Married, one daughter. Interested in photography, sport, modern music and the English countryside.

Jocelyn Semper Born in Beverley, Yorkshire, lives in Clacton-on-Sea, Essex. Student. Enjoys music and walking. Involved in voluntary work.

Howard Sergeant Born in Walton-on-Thames, Surrey. Freelance writer/editor/critic. Won the 1979 Henry Shore Award for Poetry, and the Dorothy Tutin Award in 1980. Maybe the most prolific independent publisher of poetry in Britain. His own poetry has appeared in a host of publications. Enjoys walking the Yorkshire Dales.

M. Beryl Shedden Born in Essex, lives in Birmingham. Housewife, mother of two children. Enjoys photography and fell-walking.

Timothy Stokes Born in Blackpool, lives in Lytham, Lancashire. Student. Enjoys listening to baroque music, reading.

Vaughan Stone Born in London, lives in Burgess Hill, Sussex. Teacher. Has contributed to a large number of publications. Father of four children. Enjoys natural history, languages, music.

Phil Streeter Born in Hastings, Sussex, lives in Romford, Essex. Minister of Religion. Has had two books published: *Ireland's Hope* and *The Fugitive*. Has seen his work published in a variety of magazines.

Kim Taplin Born in Oxford, lives in Southampton. Quality control manager. Married, one baby daughter. Member of The Greek Institute and The Referees' Association. Enjoys soccer, Eastern Orthodox theology and practice, and writing.

R. S. Thomas Born in Cardiff, lives in Pwllheli, North Wales. Poet/literary critic/editor. Clergyman. One of the most widely published and popular poets in Britain. His books include *Poetry for Supper, Tares, The Bread of Truth, Frequencies* and *Not That He Brought Flowers*. Has been awarded a Welsh Arts Council Literature Prize.

Phil Thomson Born in Paisley, Scotland, lives in Sutton Coldfield, West Midlands. Graphic designer, reviewer and lyricist. Married, one daughter. Co-writer of the musical work, *The Virgin*, which was broadcast on BBC Radio 1 at Christmas 1981. His book, *Listening for Clouds*, published in 1972.

Ian Todd Born and lives in Gloucester. Calculations assistant. Awarded prizes at the Stroud Festival 1972, 1973. Married. Enjoys the guitar, chess and rugby football.

Margaret Tufton Born in Norfolk, lives in Hanley Castle, Worcestershire. Part-time teacher/housewife, mother of four children. Her book, *Afloat in this Broad Night*, published in 1977. Her work included in *Blue Remembered Hills*, an anthology of Worcestershire poets, published in 1981. Enjoys walking, gardening, travel and reading. Is working on a novel.

Chris Walton Born in Leicester, lives in Birmingham. Minister of Religion. Married with three children. Lists his 'absorbing interest' as 'urban mission'.

Alex Warner Born in Middlesex, lives in Dukinfield, Cheshire. Unemployed. His poetry has appeared in magazines.

Nigel Watson Born in Hungerford, Berkshire, lives in Macclesfield, Cheshire. Social worker. Married. Enjoys drawing, painting, pottery and editing a church magazine.

Jeffery Wheatley Born in Epsom, Surrey, lives in Guildford, Surrey. Business economist. Books: *As the Hard Red Sand* and *Prince Arthur.* Has contributed to a variety of magazines. Interests include ornithology and music.

Dick Williams Born Newtown, Powys, lives in Warrington, Cheshire. Clergyman. Author and broadcaster. Books: *The Gospels in Scouse, God Thoughts, Prayers for Today's Church, Portrait of a Diocese, God Facts.*

Susan Williams Born in London, lives in Warrington. Teacher. Married to Dick, they have three children. Susan's work has appeared in many magazines. Broadcasts frequently. Interested in photography.

Robert Winnett Born in London, lives in Southampton. Clerk in Holy Orders. Books: *Divorce and Remarriage in Anglicanism*; *The Church and Divorce*; *Peter Browne, Provost, Bishop, Metaphysician.* Vice-president of The Johnson Society of London.

Veronica Zundel Born in Coventry, lives in London. Freelance writer/editor. Has written widely including contributions to *The Lion Book of Christian Poetry.* Her work has appeared in various publications. Member of the Board of Directors of the Arts Centre Group, London.